HOLLYWOOD WIT

Other humorous quotation books from Prion

Rosemarie Jarski

*Wisecracks – Great lines from classic
Hollywood movies*
*Shall I Compare Thee? – A witty collection
of quotable similes*

Des MacHale

Wit
More Wit
Yet More Wit
Wit – The Last Laugh
Wit Rides Again

Aubrey Dillon-Malone

The Cynic's Dictionary

Stephen Robins

The Importance of Being Idle

Michelle Lovric

Women's Wicked Wit

HOLLYWOOD WIT

Classic Off-screen
Quips & Quotes

Rosemarie Jarski

PRION

TO MUM, A TRUE SUPERSTAR

First published in 2000 in Great Britain by
Prion Books Limited
Imperial Works
Perren Street
London NW5 3ED
www.prionbooks.com

British Library Cataloguing in Publication Data.
A catalogue record for this book is available from the
British Library

ISBN 1-85375-385-8

All pictures courtesy of Vintage Magazine
and the Ronald Grant Archive

Printed and bound in Great Britain
by Creative Print and Design, Wales

CONTENTS

INTRODUCTION

In *LA STORY*, STEVE MARTIN REMARKS TO HIS NEW YOUNG girlfriend that her breasts feel a bit weird. "Yeah, I'm sorry," she says, "that's because they're real."

There you have it. Hollywood in a nutshell—or a D-cup: a place where the real seems more phony than the phony and the phony seems more real than the real. In this topsy-turvy town, where reality is flipped on its head, fiction is flaunted as fact, and lies are the common currency, can we ever know the truth?

The truth, as they say, is out there, and one way to get at it is to look at Hollywood through the lens of wit. Wit places Hollywood under an X-ray instead of the usual spotlight. It cuts through the hype, schmaltz and bullshit which obscure the truth. It strips away the phony silicone and reveals the real silicone underneath.

This collection brings together off-screen wit from the earliest days of Hollywood to the present. It does not try to be comprehensive. In the spirit of Sam Goldwyn's rallying cry, "Let's have some new clichés," some fustily familiar lines have ended up on the cutting-room floor to give promising newcomers a share of the limelight.

Not that old Hollywood favorites are overlooked: Groucho Marx, W.C. Fields, Cary Grant, Bette Davis, Joan Crawford...the cast list reads like an agent's wet dream. All the talents and egos who make up the Hollywood movie-making machine are here: hotshots, flesh-peddlers, hams and hacks—only in Hollywood they give themselves names like "producer," "agent," "actor," and "screenwriter."

It was the hacks, or, rather, screenwriters, who pioneered Hollywood wit. During the late 1920s some of the sharpest wit-slingers in the east headed west, lured by Hollywood lucre. The prospect of easy money and easy living is encapsulated in the famous cable sent in 1926 by Herman Mankiewicz to Ben Hecht:

WILL YOU ACCEPT THREE HUNDRED PER

WEEK TO WORK FOR PARAMOUNT
PICTURES ★ ALL EXPENSES PAID ★
THE THREE HUNDRED IS PEANUTS ★
MILLIONS ARE TO BE GRABBED OUT HERE
AND YOUR ONLY COMPETITION IS IDIOTS ★
DON'T LET THIS GET AROUND.

It was an offer Hecht could not afford to resist. He had just been fired from his reporter's job on a Chicago tabloid for writing an unacceptable headline for a story about a dentist who assaulted a patient in the dental chair: DENTIST FILLS WRONG CAVITY.

Hecht's irreverence was a quality shared by his fellow Hollywood writing recruits. Some, like him, had perfected their comic skills in the wised-up world of newspapers, others in the bitchy Broadway theater or the cut-throat atmosphere around the Algonquin Round Table. All were funny, fast, incisive and uninhibited. All were deeply cynical. The tone and tenor of Hollywood wit were set.

The California sunshine did nothing to mellow writers' cynicism. If anything, it grew more caustic. In the pecking order of the studio system, writers ranked about a notch below hairdressers. "Schmucks with Underwoods," Jack Warner called them. Warner and his fellow producers regarded writers with a mixture of suspicion and derision because, as William Goldman put it, "they never quite knew what writers did and they all knew the alphabet so they thought they could write too."

In their many battles with the studios, writers knew their best weapon was a sharpened tongue. Screenwriter, Norman Krasna, put his to good use in resolving a long-standing feud with legendary mogul, Harry Cohn. Cohn was the self-styled "biggest bug in the manure pile." He had gotten Krasna cheap and put him on a long-term contract. Krasna felt he was underpaid and wanted to quit his job and return to New York. Every day, he'd make a point of insulting the tyrant in an effort to get himself fired. The constant abuse made Cohn fume but he was damned if he was going to give in to "a hired pencil." In a last ditch attempt, Krasna took out a full page ad in the *Hollywood Reporter* in which he printed his will and at the end he added this rider: "When I die, I want to be cremated and my ashes thrown in Harry Cohn's face." That got him fired.

This story has been told, with slight variations, by dozens more denizens of Tinseltown. Harry Kurnitz, Charlie MacArthur and Garson Kanin are among those who have laid claim to it. That's the thing about Hollywood: everyone claims credit for a great story or a great line. So when they all swear on their cosmetic surgeon's life, they said it, who do you believe?

The compiler of this collection operated a foolproof attribution system: if in doubt, Tallulah said it. A bisexual, alcoholic, drug-addicted, nymphomaniac exhibitionist, Tallulah Bankhead made the Courtney Loves and Drew Barrymores of today look like convent girls. Tallulah was the original poster gal for bad behavior. She really thought there was nothing she couldn't say or do, so she often said or did it. She peed in front of Eleanor Roosevelt; she cartwheeled knickerless across a hotel lobby ("I was a natural blonde and wanted to prove it"); and when a renowned Member of Parliament and his wife were dining at the Savoy, she sashayed up to their table and declared, "What's the matter, dahling, don't you recognize me with my clothes on?" Her shameless antics shocked even Mae West—no slouch herself in the devilry department. Mae may have put the sin into cinema, but it was Tallulah who put the rage into outrageous.

Mae and Tallulah are two actors who were even funnier off the screen than on it. The same cannot be said for most actors. When Rock Hudson said, "I need a script to order a sandwich," you not only wonder who wrote that line for him but you know he spoke for the majority of actors, past and present. Without a script, very few actors cut the comic mustard. They may, like the rest of us, have the occasional lucky inspiration, but "witty" and "actor" are, for the most part, mutually exclusive terms.

The reason why there are so few wits among actors is that to be witty you need a sense of your own absurdity. You need to be able to laugh at youself. In other words, you need a sense of humor. Among Hollywood actors, that is something scarcer than a real breast on a starlet.

Actors are too self-obsessed to cultivate a sense of humor. The average actor's ego is the size of a planet. Take Alfred Lunt and Lynn Fontanne. They were a husband and wife acting team from the frontier days of Hollywood. In 1931 they co-starred in a movie called The Guardsman. Fontanne went to see the rushes, and came out gutted. "Alfred, Alfred!" she cried, "We're ruined. You photograph without lips, and I come out wrinkled and old-looking and ugly, and I lisp and waddle like a hippo. I garble my lines, I look fat, my hair's a fright, I sound awful." But as she started to sob, Lunt murmured, "No lips, eh?"

It makes you wish Dennis Pennis had been around in the thirties to prick the pomposity of Mr Lunt. (Imagine what fun he'd have with the name, for a start.) To the uninitiated, Dennis Pennis is the alter-ego of comedian, Robert Kaye. In the guise of a bespectacled orange-haired nerd, he goes around sticking the comic jackboot into the tenderest parts of stars i.e. their egos. Pennis ambushes his stellar quarry at galas and premières but instead of indulging them with the usual brown-nosing, he hits them with the thing they least expect: the truth. So, to Hugh Grant: "Which particular tree do you base your acting on?" To Demi Moore: "If it wasn't gratuitous and it was tastefully done, would you consider keeping your clothes on for a movie?" And to Steve Martin: "Why aren't you funny any more?" This is wit at its most offensive, most merciless—and most hilarious. Not only that, it is wit-as-a-public-service: Dennis Pennis says out loud what many of us are thinking but would never have the nerve to say, least of all to a star's face.

Some may feel Pennis goes too far. You cringe at the cruelty to the victims even as you snicker at the precision of the wit. But rest your consciences. You should never feel sorry for stars. They are more famous than you; they are better looking than you; they own more Lear Jets than you and frankly, they don't need your pity. As P.J. O'Rourke said, "You can't shame or humiliate modern celebrities. What used to be called shame and humiliation is now called publicity."

Stars have publicity all wrapped up. Today, because there are so many newspapers, magazines, and TV entertainment shows all vying for "the exclusive" interview with the same actors, it is the movie stars—via their Borgia-trained agents—who call the shots. Increasingly, they dictate the agenda in all contacts with the media. They demand copy approval for all interviews in newspapers and magazines (Julia Roberts did with Notting Hill, as did Tom Cruise with Legs Wide Open, I mean Eyes Wide Shut). Either that, or they demand all stories about them be written by pre-approved "safe" writers i.e. suck-ups with pens full of whitewash. Given such restrictive practices, is it any wonder most star profiles you read today are about as witty as a weather report?

Journalists who don't toe the star-line risk being black-listed. Joe Queenan, the P.J. O'Rourke of movies, had the temerity to slag off Streisand and was frozen out by Hollywood. (His sin was to dispute the fact that Ms Streisand could convincingly play the part of a $500-a-night hooker in a movie: "For a girl answering the general physical description of Barbra Streisand," he averred, "$85-a-night was more in the general price range. Room included.") Queenan's profile-writing career, post-Streisand-putdown, is neatly summed up by the title he gave his must-read book: *If You're Talking to Me, Your Career Must be in Trouble.*

Queenan's British counterpart is Lynn Barber, a journalist who specializes in cutting uppity celebs down to size. 'The Demon Barber' was taken on by *Vanity Fair* magazine to profile Hollywood's showbiz elite, but on her very first sortie behind stellar-lines she inadvertently offended Nick Nolte (she never found out how), stars closed ranks, and she, too, got the Hollywood cold shoulder. She left *Vanity Fair* shortly thereafter.

Stars may hate them, but kickass journalists like Queenan and Barber should be cherished. They are the antidote to the ever-increasing number of kissass lickspittles whose starstruck gushings saturate so much of the media today. Without the authentic voice of skepticism they represent, we are stranded in a synthetic *Hello!*-style world full of shiny, happy people living shiny, happy lives which may be mildly amusing in a postmodern way but is no substitute for genuine wit.

The endless litany of lies makes you wonder, how on earth do stars get away with it? And the answer is: because they can. We let them. We collude in their mendacity, whether unconsciously or not, because we don't want to know that our idols have feet of clay. Breasts of silicone, lips of collagen, brains of sawdust we accept, admire, embrace, adore, but feet of clay? No way. We don't want to let daylight in on the magic.

It would be misleading to imply that suppression of the truth about stars is something new. When the star system was still in place, controls on what could and could not be made public were equally rigorous. The only difference was that under the old regime, it was the studios who controlled the stars. Studio press offices fed hundreds of newspapers, dozens of fan magazines and platoons of press agents with phony stories about stars.

Two of the most powerful voices during Hollwood's heyday belonged to newspaper columnists, Hedda Hopper and Louella Parsons. These two harpies turned gossip into a blood sport. At their height, they had a combined readership estimated at 75 million. With one flick of their poison nibs, they could make or break careers. "Any dirt?" was Parsons' favorite way to open a conversation. As the wife of a doctor specializing in venereal diseases who also happened to be the studio physician at 20th Century Fox, Louella was privy to a laundry-load of Tinseltown's dirtiest secrets.

Parsons' arch rival was Hedda Hopper. When she trashed Joan Bennett in print, the disgruntled actress sent her a hat box containing a live skunk. Hedda graciously thanked the actress in her column the next day, and announced that she had christened it "Joan". Another time, Merle Oberon fronted up to her, demanding to know why she kept writing such spiteful things about her. Hedda smiled sweetly and patted the star's arm, "Bitchery, dear. Sheer bitchery."

Bitchcraft has achieved the level of art in Hollywood (so at least something has). All that naked ambition and easy money make it a hotbed of backbiting and betrayals—the sort of shenanigans that gets wit-addicts' funny bones itching in anticipation of a fix. Dispiritingly, much of the juiciest dirt is dished behind electrified fences, its public expression stifled by fear.

Fear is what runs Hollywood. Everyone who's anyone is paranoid. And "just because you're paranoid doesn't mean the bastards aren't out to get you," Lorenz Hart reminds us. Popularity counts as much as talent in a town where even mortal enemies will swear in public they want to have each other's babies. It's almost Japanese, the importance placed there on "saving face." Stardom is contingent upon being liked; celebrities, by definition, have to care what others think of them. Truth is constantly being sacrificed on the altar of image.

The fact that it is more and more difficult to get stars to tell the truth actually matters less and less these days. That's because the mystique is shifting away from star glamour and romance to far hotter topics.

Like money. In Hollywood, money talks, and what it says is fast becoming of more interest than what stars say. There is now as much interest in how much stars get paid as how often they get laid; Tom Cruise's salary is as sexy as his sex-life. Time was, film grosses were confined to the trade papers; now they're trumpeted from all corners of the media. For every picture released, we're clued up on the opening grosses, weekly grosses, monthly grosses, and closing grosses—even if we haven't the faintest notion what grosses are. The day can't be far away when instead of releasing the movie, studios just release the movie ledger sheet.

This money-mania is a reflection of what's happening right now in Hollywood. Movies are not the point anymore; it's all about the deal. The deal-makers are corporate types who, "are into pulling down $500,000 a year and fucking bimbos like shooting antelope in Africa", as David Thomson delicately puts it. So, not a lot of time for wit there.

Not a lot of time for wit on the "creative" side either. Big-hitters like James Cameron and George Lucas are never going to be mistaken for Oscar Wilde—at least, not until they come up with a special effect that can turn humorless jerks into funny guys.

In this buck 'n' fuck culture, wit is dead—or so you'd think. Miraculously, the maverick voice of wit can still be heard. It can be heard in the shape of anyone with the guts to tell it like it is. And in telling it like it is they reveal a Hollywood that is not only funnier than any faked-up fantasy; it is also more human, more genuinely moving and infinitely more seductive. Who needs silicone?

Rosemarie Jarski

Written on location in London, England,
and Los Angeles, USA

SETTING THE SCENE

HOLLYWOOD

Hollywood is a place where people from Iowa
mistake each other for stars.

Fred Allen

Hollywood's where you spend more than you make,
on things you don't need, to impress people you
don't like.

Ken Murray

Hollywood—that's where they give Oscars to people
like Charlton Heston for acting.

Shirley Knight

You can take all the sincerity in Hollywood, stuff it in
the navel of a fruit fly and still have room for three
caraway seeds and a producer's heart.

Fred Allen

Strip away the phony tinsel of Hollywood and you
find the real tinsel underneath.

Oscar Levant

Everything you hear about Hollywood is true—
including the lies.

Orson Welles

Nobody in Hollywood is innocent.

Cary Grant

SETTING THE SCENE

In Hollywood film circles, everybody lies, but it doesn't really matter because nobody listens.

Jim Backus

In Hollywood it's not how you play the game, it's how you place the blame.

Don Simpson

Never explain in this town. Deny.

Herman Mankiewicz

If I had stayed in Hollywood, I would have killed myself. Or someone would have done it for me.

Piper Laurie

You're no one in Hollywood unless someone wants you dead.

Bernie Brillstein

Hollywood is not only dog eat dog, it's dog doesn't return other dog's phonecalls.

Woody Allen

There are only two types of animal who roam in the Hollywood jungle. Those who do the fucking and those who get fucked. You just try to ensure you're one of the former for they'll shaft you in every orifice they can find, then they'll cut you open and fuck the wound.

Bruce Robinson

Hollywood is like a 500lb gorilla. What it wants for Christmas, it gets.

Chris Kennedy

Hollywood is a place where your best friend will plunge a knife into your back and then call the police to tell them that you are carrying a concealed weapon.

George Frazier

Hollywood is a place where they shoot too many pictures and not enough actors.

Walter Winchell

Hollywood people are very strange. They all seem to have fronts and no backs. They're just like the sets.

Brandon de Wilde

People in Hollywood never speak from the heart; they speak from the script, with the slightly apologetic wryness that comes from having expected a late polish which did not arrive in time.

David Thomson

I took my road test in Los Angeles, and I almost crashed into a parked car. But I still passed with a high enough score to be an instructor. That tells you something about Hollywood.

Jon Cryer

Los Angeles is full of pale imitations of Pamela
Anderson and worse still, Pamela Anderson herself.

Lisa Marchant

Living in Hollywood is like living in a lit cigar butt.

Phyllis Diller

Living in Hollywood is like wearing Fiberglass
underwear—interesting but painful.

Robin Williams

There's nothing wrong with Hollywood that six first-
class funerals couldn't cure.

Anon 1930s

I've committed the unpardonable sin in Hollywood.
I've grown up.

Nelson Eddy

I've had several years in Hollywood and I still think
the movie heroes are in the audience.

Wilson Mizner

No one "goes Hollywood"—they were that way before
they came here. Hollywood just exposed it.

Ronald Reagan

Hollywood...where everyone's a genius until he's lost
his job.

Erskine Johnson

A combination kosher deli and El Dorado.

Dorothy Parker

Geniuses, geniuses everywhere I turn! If only there was some talent!

Henri Bernstein

God felt sorry for actors, so he gave them a place in the sun with a swimming pool. The price they had to pay was to surrender their talent.

Cedric Hardwicke

The smartest, most gifted people in the world live in Hollywood. Those who knock the town, 1) never made it, 2) have no chance to make it, or 3) made it and blew it.

Billy Wilder

The only town where you can die of encouragement.

Pauline Kael

Of all the Christbitten places and business on the two hemispheres Hollywood is the last curly kink on the pig's tail.

Stephen Vincent Benét

Hollywood, land of contrasts: where any day you can see the very rich rubbing shoulders with the rich.

Kenneth Tynan

Hollywood isn't anything like Hollywood.

Will Smith

Living in Hollywood is a contradiction in terms.

Kathy Lette

Hollywood is a sewer—with service from the Ritz-Carlton.

Wilson Mizner

A town that has to be seen to be disbelieved.

Walter Winchell

The true and original arse-hole of creation.

H. L. Mencken

A trip through a sewer in a glass-bottomed boat.

Wilson Mizner

A miners' camp in Lotus Land.

F. Scott Fitzgerald

Sodom-on-the-Sea.

Anon

Dottyville-on-the-Pacific.

W.C. Fields

Paradise with a lobotomy.

Neil Simon

Disneyland restaged by Dante.

Robin Williams

A great place to live—if you're an orange.

Fred Allen

California is a tragic country—like Palestine, like every Promised Land.

Christopher Isherwood

LA is a big hard-boiled city with no more personality than a paper cup.

Raymond Chandler

Not knowing the name of a single hotel in Los Angeles, I asked the studio executive where I should stay. "How about the Château Marmont?" he said. "Is that good?" I asked. "Is that good?" he repeated, somewhat stunned. "Well, John Belushi died there."

Jay McInerney

The rudest thing I've heard anyone say about Los Angeles is that it's populated by air-heads and I'd find that conversation is something of a lost art. I'd love to know what kind of conversations they imagine I have in Leicester.

Leanda de Lisle

The City of Angels—where every cockroach has a screenplay and even the winos wear roller skates. It's that kind of town.

Ian Sholes

Too many freeways, too much sun, abnormality taken normally, pink stucco houses and pink stucco consciences.

Clancy Sigal

The flowers out there smell like dirty old dollar bills.

Dorothy Parker

The fruit has no taste, and the women have no milk
in their breasts.

Don Marquis

I love Los Angeles. I love Hollywood. They're
beautiful. Everybody's plastic. I want to be plastic.

Andy Warhol

There is that deep-seated notion that we are all
phonies in Hollywood. Making stacks of money and
no taxes. Banging all those tall dames. Indoor and
outdoor pools. Sixteen in help. All driving fancy cars.
Well, it's all true. Eat your heart out.

Billy Wilder

Beverly Hills has got a slum area, and it's called the
rest of the world.

Bob Hope

Greer Garson's bathroom was all done in pink marble,
and had a huge glass wall which opened onto a
private garden. It was the biggest production for the
smallest audience that Hollywood ever achieved.

George Sanders

That's what God would have done if he'd had money.

**Herman Mankiewicz , on being shown
around a Beverley Hills estate**

Hollywood's all right. It's the pictures that are bad.

Orson Welles

I once asked a fellow-screenwriter where the Beverly Hills set got their groceries, and he said, "Doggy bags."

Keith Waterhouse

The Church of the Good Shepherd in Beverly Hills is known locally as Our Lady of the Cadillacs.

Jay Leno

Guys who can't tie their own shoelaces are driving around Beverly Hills in $80,000 cars.

James Woods

If you stay in Beverly Hills too long you become a Mercedes.

Robert Redford

Hollywood provided the sort of luxury that only exists today for the sons of Latin-American dictators.

Groucho Marx

I look upon going to Hollywood as a mission behind enemy lines. You parachute in, set up the explosion, then fly out before it goes off.

Robert Redford

Basically, Hollywood is like high school with money.

Joel Silver

There's great respect for the dead in Hollywood, but none for the living.

Errol Flynn

All I got from 25 years in Hollywood is three lousy
ex-husbands.

Ava Gardner

Hollywood's a place where they'll pay you $50,000
for a kiss and 50 cents for your soul. I know because
I turned down the first offer enough and held out for
the 50 cents.

Marilyn Monroe

It's a shame to take this country away from the
rattlesnakes.

D.W. Griffith

Hollywood will be a tourist spot like Tombstone,
Arizona, before the century's done.

Ben Hecht, 1957

MOVIESPEAK

The three most common phrases to be heard in
Hollywood are: "The check is in the mail," "The
Jaguar is in the garage," and "I promise I won't
come in your mouth."

Andrew Yule

Character actress. An actress too ugly to be called a
leading lady.

Kathy Burke

Supporting players. Those Nearly Men and Women in Hollywood whose careers are devoted to helping inferior talents collect larger pay checks than them.

Mark Steyn

Belly Laugh. Your own gag.

Snicker. What the collaborator contributes to the script.

Preview. The beginning of a studio shake-up.

Groucho Marx

The words "loyalty" and "friendship," in Hollywood terms, roughly mean "We've made money together, and our current spouses like each other."

Celia Brady

Never refer to "the script." It's "the piece," "the play," "the work"—and I even heard one producer call it "the vision."

Laura Baum

Hollywood. Rocky XXII

Car-park movie. A movie you forget the moment you get out of the movie-theater and into the car park.

Air-conditioning movie. A movie you go to see purely to escape the summer heat.

Crowd-pleasing movie. A terrible movie but, guess what, it made lots of money.

Classic. Anything in black and white.

Creative concept. An idea.

12

High Concept. Low Concept.

Action. Violence.

Dahling. I haven't a clue who the fuck you are.

To pitch. To grovel shamelessly.

To network. To spread disinformation.

To freelance. To collect unemployment.

Anon

Friend. I've talked to him on the phone, but we've never met.

Good Friend. We had a chance meeting once.

Great Friend. Ran into him at a social event.

My New Best Friend. Someone who will make me a lot of money.

Good in a room. Able to schmooze, drop names, and mention popular vacation spots without letting on that you can't afford to refill your gas tank.

I love to work with young writers. I can't pay you anything.

I didn't love the script. It made me sick.

It's a movie. Somebody might possibly make this, but it won't be me.

We're on the same page. Hey, that's a good idea; I'm going to say it was mine.

It's cute. Next.

See ya! Not in this lifetime.

Gillis & Mayhew

How much will I be allowed to be involved? Who can I control?

Let me talk to my people. No.

He's the next big action star. He looks great stripped to the waist. He can't act, but don't worry, the noise and the explosions will cover it up.

He's the next John Travolta. We're hoping he'll make a big comeback.

I enjoyed working with him. He wasn't the total bastard he's been made out to be.

Creative differences. She/He refused to sleep with me.

It's very much the writer's film. I couldn't understand a fucking word of it.

It's important. It's worthy and it bored the pants off me.

We can fix it in the editing room. We're fucked and it's too late to do anything about it.

I never read the critics. They never write about me.

I don't believe in awards. I wasn't even nominated.

It doesn't matter that I didn't win. The nomination is all that counts and knowing I have the respect of my peers. There is no justice. There is no God. Fuck you all.

The quotes were taken out of context. I'm in big trouble now that it's out.

We wish him well in future endeavors. Quick, change
the locks on his office-door and have security carry
him out.

Anon

He's underrated. Everyone thought he was dead.
Film Noir. Originally a low-budget film made purely
for money, now a recently discovered masterpiece.
Blockbuster. The promotional budget is greater than
the cost of making the film.
Exclusive Interview. His new film is out soon, so Tom
Cruise's PR woman finally agreed.
Kooky. Unfunny and unattractive American actress.

Malcolm Burgess

EARLY DAYS

I don't remember any silent days in motion pictures
—the directors always yelled.

Arthur Baer

In 1912, Adolph Zukor wanted me to make six pictures
a year for the Famous Players. "Adolph," I pleaded,
"there isn't that much talent in the world."

Edwin Porter

Adding sound to movies would be like putting lipstick on the Venus de Milo.

Mary Pickford

Motion pictures need dialogue as much as Beethoven symphonies need lyrics.

Charlie Chaplin

For the love scenes in my first Hollywood silent picture, Dark Angel, I spoke in my own language, Hungarian, and my co-star, Ronald Colman, chatted about cricket and kippers.

Vilma Banky

The arrival of talking movies will in no way affect my favorite motion picture actors—the horses.

Don Herold

The talkies made me sound as if I'd been castrated.

Tallulah Bankhead

THE FILM

MAKING MOVIES

Film is a collaborative art: bend over.

David Mamet

A team effort is a lot of people doing what I say.

Michael Winner

I'm Il Duce. I'm sure Picasso never asked his art dealer, "What do you think? Should I stop using gray?"

Nicolas Winding Refn, director

In the movie business, the director is God—but unfortunately the actors are atheists.

Brad Lucas

I consider myself just another member of the crew. The highest paid member of the crew.

William Friedkin, director

A movie is never any better than the stupidest man connected with it. Most often this distinction belongs to the producer.

Ben Hecht

It's really no fun to work with sane people, people who have a set way of doing things.

John Cassevetes

Movies are like wars. The guy who becomes an expert is the guy who doesn't get killed.

Robert Towne

Most directors who have been around for a while acquire a gaunt, soul-scarred look associated with fighter pilots who have survived a war.

Jack Cardiff

Life in the movie business is like the beginning of a new love affair: it's full of surprises and you're constantly getting fucked.

David Mamet

Film-making has now reached the same stage as sex—it's all technique and no feeling.

Penelope Gilliat

When I'm making a movie I become partially celibate. I get into the routine of fucking my movie. I become mad Dr Frankenstein, with test tubes and electrical sparks, creating a living organism from dead parts.

Steven Spielberg

If we made cars the way they make movies, we would all be pedestrians.

Kurt Luedtke

Making a film is like trying to write *War and Peace* in a bumper car in an amusement park.

Stanley Kubrick

You don't make a movie, the movie makes you.

Jean-Luc Godard

Making a film is a cross between a circus, a military campaign, a nightmare, an orgy and a high.

Norman Mailer

The way to make a film is to begin with an earthquake and work up to a climax.

Cecil B. De Mille

Shooting a film is like taking a stagecoach ride in the Old West. At first you look forward to a nice trip. Later you just hope to reach your destination.

François Truffaut

Making a movie is a crazy time. It's painting a picture on a railroad track with the train getting closer.

Dustin Hoffman

Making a movie is like discovering you have a fatal illness - you live and love twice as deeply. Then it's over and you shed it like a snake sheds its skin.

Angelina Jolie

Making movies is easy. You just turn the camera on.
And then, if you go into commercial filming, it's
even easier because people do it all for you. They
really do.

Andy Warhol

Movie-making is pointing the camera at beautiful
women.

François Truffaut

Movies aren't made, they're remade.

Irving Thalberg

What's the toughest thing about film-making?
Putting in the little holes.

Mel Brooks

Don't do research. It can only cripple the fine art of
invention.

Orson Welles

We never do any research. Ethan says research is for
sissies.

Joel Coen

When I enter the studios—be it in Hollywood or
London—and the heavy doors close behind me, there
is no difference. A salt mine is a salt mine.

Alfred Hitchcock

Ten million dollars' worth of intricate and highly ingenious machinery functioning elaborately to put skin on baloney.

George Jean Nathan

—How long should the film be?
—How long is it good?

Director and Nicholas Schenck

A film set, as Orson Welles was first to say, is the most wonderful electric train set a boy could ever be given. What he failed to add was that most of the time it doesn't work.

Frank Pearson

There are no rules in film-making. Only sins. And the cardinal sin is dullness.

Frank Capra

Style just gets you 7 minutes of attention.

Michael Mann, director

Of course there must be subtleties in filmmaking. Just make sure you make them obvious.

Billy Wilder

Prepare for the worst. Always a good thing to prepare for, among actors.

Joseph L. Mankiewicz

The sitting around on set is awful, but I always figure that's what they pay me for. The acting I do for free.

Edward G. Robinson

Don't come too close, you'll see through my talent.

Ralph Richardson to a lighting cameraman

Dining-table scenes are probably the most difficult thing to film next to war scenes.

Ang Lee

I always say that the most difficult things to photograph are dogs, babies, motorboats, Charles Laughton (God rest his soul), and method actors.

Alfred Hitchcock

If any one thing is wrong with the movie industry today, it is the unrelenting effort to astonish.

Clive James

Renny Harlin never really spoke to me on Cutthroat Island. He spent a lot of his time just finding new ways to blow things up.

Matthew Modine

I'm not crazy about talking vacuum cleaners and explosions.

Richard Sylbert

Cinemascope? The next time I write a poem, I shall use a larger piece of paper.

Jean Cocteau

The widescreen format is only good for the love story of two dachshunds.

Billy Wilder

You can have all the high-tech equipment in the world, but what matters is who is turning the knobs. Like two concert pianists playing the same piano, it's down to personality.

Sydney Samuelson

—Does new technology mean you're going to start making original motion pictures starring dead movie stars?
—We don't think of them as being dead. They're only resting between jobs. They're just respiratorally challenged.

Reporter and Hollywood Lawyer

Morphing, anyone can do it. Yesterday's mind-boggling device becomes today's techno-yawn.

John Bruno, special effects wizard

How could director Ronald Neame spend almost $17 million on Meteor and then the best special effect is Sean Connery's toupée?

Rona Barrett

Sharon Stone turned the simple act of parting her legs into the screen's greatest special effect since Charlton Heston parted the Red Sea in The Ten Commandments.

Steve Rebello on Basic Instinct

Nothing essential has been added to the art of the motion picture since D.W. Griffith.

René Clair

A film is like a parachute jump. If it doesn't open, you're dead.

Robert Evans

Distribution is a freemasonry like the kitchens of a restaurant. They have deep, dark secrets. I have never yet been able to discover how much it costs to distribute a film.

Alfred Hitchcock

Drugs, ship's chandlering and film distribution are the three dirtiest businesses I know. There is a culture of film distribution that is no different from peddling drugs.

Rolf de Heer

How do films get made? There's no rational answer. Do you realize how many people in the film business don't even go to the movies?

David Picker

There's only one reason why films get made: GREED.

Alan Parker, cartoon caption

Making a film is like sperm. Only one in a million makes it.

Claude Lelouch

GENRE

There are four things to stay away from in movies: boats and water, animals, kids, and futurism.

Fred Gallo

You've got to keep surprising them. Always come out of another hole.

Noël Coward to David Lean

If you see a man come through a doorway, it means nothing. If you see him coming through a window–that is at once interesting.

Billy Wilder

You can't spring a new plot on an audience the first time and expect it to go. It takes a movie audience years to get used to a new plot.

Will Rogers

Find a formula and milk it until it moos with pain.

Dorothy Parker

Hollywood has no more notion of telling a story than a blind puppy has of composing a symphony.

George Bernard Shaw

There are only six basic plots. Frankenstein and My Fair Lady are really the same story.

William Holden

All great American films are love stories between two men.

Brad Lucas

All American films boil down to, "I love you, dad."

Ian Hislop

All movies are westerns. You put the hare in front of the hounds and let the hounds chase the hare.

Sam Peckinpah

No gals, no gags, no chance.

Michael Todd

When in doubt, have two guys come through the door with guns.

Raymond Chandler

What we're watching at home is dictated by tastes in the Far East and South-East Asia. You don't have to know the language to know something is exploding and to enjoy that spectacle.

Meryl Streep

I have a surefire idea for combining serious Oscar material with chick-flick romantic comedy. It can't lose. I'm gonna call it, Saving Meg Ryan.

Libby Gelman-Waxner

Six films I made with Don Ameche and in every one of them my voice was deeper than the plot.

Alice Faye

A plot at last.

Epitaph for a screenwriter

All these movies I made are being remade. I just wish they could remake me.

Michael Caine

The title of Alan Bennett's stage play is *The Madness of George III* but they changed it for the film to The Madness of King George. It was thought American audiences might see a film called The Madness of George III and think they'd missed parts one and two.

Lisa Marchant

I hear Stallone's going to do Rocky VI. Don't worry if you miss it, you can just watch Rocky III twice.

Jay Leno

A long, difficult word can be a real positive in a movie title. Trust me—soon you'll think of Armageddon like Haagen-Däzs.

Joe Roth, chairman, Disney Studio, 1998

I was once sent a script combining *Wuthering Heights* and *Jane Eyre*, cunningly titled, Jane Heights.

Cameron Mackintosh

You can be pretty sure that any film with "bikini" in its title is a) going to show you some wobbly flesh, b) going to try to make you laugh and, c) fail.

Tim Healey

City Slickers was a hit all over the world—except in France. I couldn't figure out why till they told me they'd changed the title to La Vie, L'Amour et Les Vaches which means, Life, Love and Cows.

Billy Crystal

The title Star Wars was an insurance policy. We calculated that there are something like $8 million worth of science fiction freaks in the USA and they will go to see absolutely anything with a title like Star Wars.

George Lucas

29

The Godfather—They should retitle it Four Funerals and a Wedding.

Steven Smith

My favorite kind of movie would be one that opened with a shot of me sitting in a rocking chair on a front porch. The rest of the picture would be what I saw.

Bing Crosby

Comedy

Tragedy is if I cut my finger. Comedy is if I walk into an open sewer and die.

Mel Brooks

All I need to make a comedy is a park, a policeman and a pretty girl.

Charlie Chaplin

Ben Turpin insisted the studio take out a policy with Lloyds of London which would pay him one million dollars if his eyes ever came uncrossed.

Mack Sennett

Confront a man in his office with a nuclear alarm, and you have a documentary. If the news reaches him in his living room, you have a drama. If it catches him in the lavatory, the result is comedy.

Stanley Kubrick

Harold Lloyd is funny from the inside.

James Agee

We never make fun of religion, politics, race or mothers. A mother never gets hit with a custard-pie. Mothers-in-law, yes. But mothers, never.

Mack Sennett

Non-participation on the part of the recipient of the pastry is the chief ingredient of the recipe for successful custard-pie throwing.

Jack Sennett

It is funnier to bend things than to break them—bend the fenders on a car in a comedy wreck, don't tear them off. In my golf game sketch, which I have been doing for years, at first I swung at the ball and broke the club. Now I bend it at a right angle.

W.C. Fields

The funniest thing about comedy is that you never know why people laugh. I know what makes them laugh, but trying to get your hands on the why is like trying to pick an eel out of a tub of water.

W.C. Fields

The difference between English and American humor is $150 a minute.

Eric Idle, 1990

The way to play comedy: Don't play it straight. Play it deadly serious.

David Zucker

31

One of the first things I noticed was that whenever I smiled or let the audience suspect how much I was enjoying myself, they didn't seem to laugh as much as usual.

Buster Keaton

Imperturbably serious, inscrutable and stubborn, Buster Keaton acts under the impulse of an irresistible power unknown to himself, comparable only to the mysterious urge that causes the birds to migrate or the avalanche to come rushing down.

Erwin Panofsky

Thanks for the warning.

Billy Wilder after watching a trailer for an unfunny comedy

Oliver Hardy's huge hands affect an elaborate grace; he has a way of ringing a doorbell which is like a courtly bow.

David Robinson

Snooty James Finlayson appeared in many of Laurel and Hardy's films, with his look of eternally tasting a spoiled pickle.

James Agee

I don't really find any silent comedians funny. I don't identify with it. I've never had to wallpaper a room while delivering a piano upstairs.

Angus Deayton

Everything is funny as long as it is happening to somebody else.

Will Rogers

Laugh at yourself first, before anyone else can.

Elsa Maxwell

We were previewing Ninotchka in Long Beach. The audience filled out the preview cards and Ernst Lubitsch read one of them out. It said, "Funniest picture I ever saw. So funny that I peed in my girl-friend's hand."

Billy Wilder

I'm not funny. What I am is brave.

Lucille Ball

The only surefire way to test out a new gag was to try it out on Zeppo. If he liked it, we threw it out.

Groucho Marx

An amateur thinks it's funny if you dress a man up as an old lady, sit him in a wheelchair, and shove the wheelchair down a slope towards an approaching car. For a pro, it's got to be a real old lady.

Groucho Marx

Robin Williams's technique is to say 500 things with a joke rhythm, and at least two of them might be funny.

Libby Gelman-Waxner

33

Laughter usually occurs when something funny has happened; that is why the death of a friend seldom evokes a chuckle, but a funny hat does.

Woody Allen

In the end, everything is a gag.

Charlie Chaplin

Whenever anyone asks me to tell them something funny I just say, "Toupée." It's all you need to say.

John Cleese

I hate jokes. I cringe when anyone tells me a joke. They always say, "You can use that in one of your scripts." I never have.

Neil Simon

When people ask me where I get my ideas from I say, "A little man in Swindon. But I don't know where he gets them from."

John Cleese

A studio executive said, "This script should be about 20% funnier." When somebody says that you want to kill them.

William Goldman

The secret of all comedy writing is—write Jewish and cast Gentile.

Robert Kaufman

I think in twenty years I'll be looked at like Bob Hope.
Doing these president jokes and golf jokes. It scares me.
Eddie Murphy

Making a funny film provides all the enjoyment of
getting your leg caught in the blades of a threshing
machine. As a matter of fact, it's not even that
pleasurable; with the threshing machine the end
comes much quicker.

Woody Allen

Costume Drama

The concept of Merchant Ivory movies is foreign to
America: there's no sex, nothing gratuitous or
violent.

Gwyneth Paltrow

Definition of a classic: a book everyone is assumed to
have read and often think they have.

Alan Bennett

The nearest thing we get to action in Emma is when
someone draws the curtains.

Doug McGrath, writer-director of Emma

So she wouldn't be available for book signings?

Anonymous executive on being told Jane Austen was dead

I grew a beard for Nero in Quo Vadis, but MGM thought
it didn't look real, so I had to wear a false one.

Peter Ustinov

I'm a genre unto myself. If a period film opens and
I'm not in it, the critics write, "And the Helena
Bonham Carter role is played by..."

Helena Bonham Carter

Jewel had a period upbringing and a period look.
She's even got period teeth.

Ang Lee

–I'd like to appear in one of those Charles Dickens
films.

–Have you read the books?

–Oh no, but I've got them all on audio tapes.

–Have you listened to them?

–Not all of them–I'm a slow listener.

Interviewer and Pamela Anderson

I'm going back to the stage. I've done all that
running round fields with straw hats on.

Imogen Stubbs

I'd rather be unemployed than do the next script
that comes in where the first thing mentioned is a
frock coat.

Rufus Sewell

Don't send me any more pictures where the hero
signs his name with a feather.

Movie exhibitor to a Hollywood studio

Musicals

A musical is a series of catastrophes ending with a
floor show.

Oscar Levant

It seems that the moment anyone gets hold of an
exclamation mark these days, he promptly sits down
and writes a musical around it.

George Jean Nathan

Oklahoma! was the first musical I ever saw where
the people were not complete idiots.

Ernst Lubitsch

Busby Berkeley production numbers look like
colonies of bacteria staging a political rally under a
microscope.

Clive James

The joy of my dancing is that you never forget it's an
eternal fertility rite.

Gene Kelly

I like to dance like sailors, fighters, steel workers. I
belonged to the sweatshirt generation. Put me in
tails and I look like a truck driver going to meet the
mayor.

Gene Kelly

I learned how to dance from learning how to fight.

James Cagney

As for my leading ladies at MGM, the hardest thing was finding dancers who could also act and sing. Most of them couldn't even say hello.

Gene Kelly

If we remade Singin' in the Rain today, when Gene Kelly sings in the rain I think he'd be looking around to make sure he wasn't going to get mugged.

Stanley Donen

—Do you think the tunes of George Gershwin will be played in a 100 years' time?
—Sure, if George is here to play them.

Reporter and Groucho Marx

I had to hit myself on the head afterwards with a small hammer to get that stupid Tomorrow song out of my head.

Ian Sholes on Annie

A musical is like another fellow's wife or sweetheart. For one man who shares his taste there are always those who wonder what he sees in her.

George Jean Nathan

Horror

Most horror films are certainly that.

Brendan Francis

I've never been in a horror film—on purpose.

Peter O'Toole

Fear is something behind you.

Slavko Vorkapich

The first scary thing I learned to do as a child was to turn off the light.

Steven Spielberg

Alfred Hitchcock is interested in making your mind, rather than your flesh, creep.

Laura Baum

Norman Bates is the Hamlet of horror roles.

Anthony Perkins

We had snakes in Raiders of the Lost Ark and bugs in Indiana Jones and the Temple of Doom. But supposedly man's greatest fear is public speaking. That'll be in our next picture.

Steven Spielberg

We're gonna sell you this seat, but you're only gonna use the edge of it.

Quentin Tarantino, promotion for Reservoir Dogs

In all Michael Winner's The Nightcomers there is hardly enough of either terror or common sense to impose on the average tufted titmouse.

Time magazine

Make a film like Rosemary's Baby? I wouldn't touch it with a five-foot Pole.

Billy Wilder

Only a terror of possible coma kept audiences awake through Surf Terror.

Alan Frank

Science Fiction

A lot of people with names like Zircona, Placenta and Tampon crawling through air vents.

Mark Lamarr

Science fiction is where actors go when they die.

Quentin Crisp

Western

It is easier to get an actor to be a cowboy than to get a cowboy to be an actor.

John Ford

A cowboy actor needs only two changes of expression—hat on and hat off.

Fred MacMurray

I always think better with a horse between my knees.

Ronald Reagan

In those silent cowboy movies, we never changed the plots, only the horses.

Texas Guinan

I made over 40 westerns. I used to lie awake nights trying to think up new ways of getting on and off a horse.

William Wyler

I started out playing the villain in Hopalong Cassidy
Westerns. I got $100 a week and all the horseshit I
could carry home.

Robert Mitchum

As I look back now, Tom Mix was as elegant on a
horse as Fred Astaire on a dance floor, and that's the
elegantest there is.

Adela Rogers St Johns

THE MOVIE MAKERS

PRODUCERS

–What's a producer?

–A guy with a desk.

Hollywood joke

The producer is the big-shot, but his real function, outside of prodigious cigar-smoking, has never been discovered.

George Sanders

The producer is an authoritarian figure who risks nothing, presumes to know public taste, and always wants to change the end of the film.

Frederico Fellini

A producer is a man who asks you a question, gives you the answer, and then tells you what's wrong with it.

Lamarr Trotti

I got a job at Metro. I wanted to write and direct but Mayer said, "No! You have to produce first. You have to crawl before you walk"–which is as good a definition of producing as I've ever heard.

Joseph L. Mankiewicz

Nobody sets out to be a producer. Most producers are failed directors–but so are most directors.

Lyle Bernard

Anyone can be a producer—all you need is a talented
friend who can write, act or direct.

Boyd Farrow

A producer is just a dog with a script in his mouth.

Peter Guber

Some are able and humane men and some are low-
grade individuals with the morals of a goat, the
artistic integrity of a slot machine, and the manners
of a floorwalker with delusions of grandeur.

Raymond Chandler

I hate all producers—except my brother. And I even
hate him, when he's acting like a producer.

Myron Selznick on his brother, David

Hollywood producers have the manners of ants at a
picnic.

Marlon Brando

Producing is a thankless task akin to hotel
management.

David Hemmings

The producer's job is to put out fires. It's crisis
management.

Lynda Obst

It's better than being a pimp.

Harry Cohn

Every putz thinks he can produce a movie. There isn't anybody who's asked me what I do who doesn't think, after I try to explain it, that they could do it too. Producing is bullshit work. It's a bunch of silly people running around trying to take credit for other people's stuff.

Art Linson

STUDIOS & MOGULS

Most movie moguls couldn't produce a urine sample.

Kathy Lette

Studio heads have foreheads by dint of electrolysis.

S.J. Perelman

One could have swung a scythe 5 feet off the ground at a gathering of those early movie moguls, without endangering any lives; several would scarcely have heard the swish.

Philip French

I've told my wife, if I ever need cardiac surgery, get me the heart of a movie mogul. It's never been used.

Jack Columbo

—How many people work at Warner Bros?
—About half.

Reporter and Julius Epstein

I can't see what Jack Warner can do with an Oscar—it can't say yes.

Al Jolson

If there's one thing I can't stand, it's yes-men. When I say no, I want you to say no, too.

Jack Warner

I don't want yes-men around me. I want everybody to tell me the truth even if it costs them their jobs.

Sam Goldwyn

Executives in Hollywood will tell you they don't like yes-men. But there are very few no-men working here.

Mark Hellinger

The first time I tried to get a movie made in the Hollywood system, my agent said to me, "There are yes lists and no lists, and you aren't even on the no list."

Alain Rudolph

For God's sake, don't say yes until I've finished talking.

Darryl F. Zanuck

Darryl Zanuck has so many yes-men following him around the studio, he ought to put out his hand when he makes a sharp turn.

Fred Allen

One time I saw Darryl Zanuck in Pamplona watching a bullfight. It started to rain. Everyone left the arena except Zanuck. He sat there, and his cigar did not go out. God does not rain on Darryl Zanuck.

Kenneth Tynan

Darryl Zanuck became obsessed with Bella Davri when she taught him that he could do it in bed, not only on a desk.

Nunnally Johnson

Any of my indiscretions were with women, not actresses.

Darryl F. Zanuck

Irving Thalberg was a sweet guy but he could piss ice water.

Eddie Mannix

To know him was to like him. Not to know him was to love him.

Bert Kalmar on Herman Mankiewicz

One famous movie executive who shall remain nameless, exposed himself to me in his office. "Mr X," I said, "I thought you were a producer not an exhibitor."

Shirley Temple

Howard Hughes would fuck a tree if it moved.

Joan Crawford

I once heard a producer say about Howard Hughes: "He's entitled to his own opinion—and as many others as money can buy."

Robert Mitchum

Selznick gave the impression that he stormed through life demanding to see the manager—and that, when the manager appeared, Selznick would hand him a 22-page memo announcing his instant banishment to Elba.

Lloyd Shearer

At least the old moguls had the courage of their convictions and the authority to act on them. Today they're terrified of making decisions. You have to have eight meetings even to order the toilet paper.

Brian Forbes

It's the real Revenge of the Nerds. Most of these guys were short, fat, ugly kids who couldn't get laid in high school. Now they're in control, and they're going to make everyone in the world pay for what the world did to them.

Joel Silver, 1987

If some of those people weren't running film studios they'd be running the Mafia. But at least in the Mafia there's some kind of loyalty to the family.

Verity Lambert, 1986

Mauschwitz.

Employees' name for the Disney Studios under Michael Eisner and Jeffrey Katzenberg

Katzenberg is the eighth dwarf—Greedy.

Alec Baldwin

If you're not willing to come in on Saturday, don't even bother coming in on Sunday.

Jeffrey Katzenberg, CEO, Disney Studios, to an employee

Angels. Angels with claws.

Anthony Minghella on Bob and Harvey Weinstein, head honchos at Miramax

It was Japanese management theory on acid.

Unnamed employee of Miramax.

I do call people "assholes." It's a term of affection to me.

Dawn Steel, movie executive

Wherever Irving Thalberg sits is always head of the table.

F.L. Collins

When I was invited to a birthday party for Mark
Canton, chief of production at Warner Brothers, I
couldn't come up with a suitable gift—what do you
give a man who wants everything?

Harold Ramis

Every day I have two choices. One is to make a series
of absolutely insane deals and the other is to make
no movies at all.

Peter Chermin, CEO, Fox Filmed Entertainment

In Hollywood today, the deal is the sex, the movie is
the cigarette.

Thom Taylor, 1999

If you're asking me, would I really work for a
Hollywood studio or would I rather stick needles in
my eyeballs, I would say pass me the needles.

Mike Leigh

The thing about Hollywood is, you have to be
grateful to be working with thieves and liars,
because the alternative is idiots.

David Ambrose

When you wake up in the morning, put on your
battle fatigues, put a gun in your right pocket, and
put a gun in your left pocket, and go to work. That's
how you survive at the studio.

Don Simpson

I haven't been able to find anybody running a studio that even knows that movies are 35mm and run at 24 frames per second.

Douglas Trumball

In The Rock, just before Nicolas Cage goes into battle he assures Sean Connery, "I'll do my best," and Connery turns on him. "Losers always whine about doing their best," he says. "Winners go home and fuck the prom queen." Words to live by. It's the Simpson-Bruckheimer-Bay philosophy in a nutshell.

Terrence Rafferty

Don Simpson pushed the envelope always, and the envelope pushed back.

Tom Pollock

I was introduced to a producer called Marvin in a Hollywood restaurant. He said, "What's your name?" I said, "John Cleese." He went back to talking for a long time with the man he was with. Then he came over to me and said, "Hey, I'm a big fan of yours."

John Cleese

When I first arrived in Hollywood, I met a studio executive who said, "Loved your work, Joe." When I asked what he had seen me in, he said, "Nothing."

Joseph Fiennes

Producing a movie can often be a blood-stained affair. But if you can figure it out, it will definitely keep your pool heated.

Art Linson

Hollywood executives only worry about making enough money to fill their own swimming pools until they get fired.

Robert Altman

Decisions are made by so many executives who come and go so fast, there's always the danger that after a year and a half you find you've been kissing the wrong ass all along.

Billy Wilder

One of the things you do when you become president of a studio is that you negotiate what happens when they fire you. Because eventually you will get fired.

Phil Alden Robinson

Firing people came as naturally as breathing to Harry Cohn, more naturally in fact.

Ben Hecht

I was a reporter before I went to Hollywood. I went from covering Al Capone to covering Harry Cohn. Cohn was by far the meanest. He used to fire people all the time—usually on Christmas Eve.

James Bacon

Howard Hughes never fired anyone. If he wanted to get rid of somebody, he'd merely put somebody else in over the guy.

Sam Bischoff

Hollywood must be the only place on earth where you can get fired by someone wearing a Hawaiian shirt and a baseball cap.

Steve Martin

The picture business can be a little trying at times, but I don't suppose working for General Motors is all sheer delight.

Raymond Chandler

Harry Cohn

I don't get ulcers. I give 'em.

Harry Cohn

You had to stand in line to hate him.

Hedda Hopper

The softest thing about him is his front teeth.

Damon Runyon

–Harry Cohn wouldn't hurt a fly.
–Not if it was buttoned up.

Studio executive and Dorothy Parker

It proves what they always say: give the public what they want to see, and they'll come out for it.

Red Skelton on the crowds at Cohn's funeral

–Can you think of anything good to say about Harry Cohn?

–He's dead.

Reporter and Rabbi Edgar Magnin at Cohn's funeral

Samuel Goldwyn

To understand Sam you must realize that he regards himself as a nation.

Lillian Hellman

He filled the room with a wonderful panic and beat at your mind like a man in front of a slot machine, shaking it for a jackpot.

Ben Hecht

Sam Goldwyn was a sensitive, creative artist with a fine sense of double-entry book-keeping.

Alexander Woollcott

The only man who could throw a seven with one dice.

Harpo Marx

I was always an independent, even when I had partners.

Sam Goldwyn

I made Wuthering Heights. William Wyler only directed it.

Sam Goldwyn

Dodsworth was a great picture. But no one wanted to see it. In droves.

Sam Goldwyn

You write with great warmth and charmth.

Sam Goldwyn to Joseph L. Mankiewicz

We'll jump off that bridge when we come to it.

Sam Goldwyn

When I want your opinion, I'll give it to you.

Sam Goldwyn

Never let the bastard back in here—unless we need him.

Sam Goldwyn

I'll give you a definite maybe.

Sam Goldwyn

I can answer you in two words, im-possible.

Sam Goldwyn

Gentlemen—include me out.

Sam Goldwyn

Louis B. Mayer

They say Louis B. Mayer is his own worst enemy. Not while I'm still alive.

Jack Warner

A bastard's bastard.

Garson Kanin

56

He charms the birds out of the trees, then shoots 'em.

Herman Mankiewicz

Louis B. Mayer's arm around your shoulder meant his hand was closer to your throat.

Jules Dassin

I told Mr Mayer I wasn't going to do any more poor scripts. He became furious and screamed, "You'll do what I tell you! Remember, we made you and we can break you!" "God made me," I said, and left Hollywood for good.

Luise Rainer

The only reason so many people showed up at his funeral was because they wanted to make sure he was dead.

Sam Goldwyn

DIRECTORS

Directors are people too short to be actors.

Josh Greenfeld

Hollywood has always been full of bartenders and waiters who want to be directors. Trouble is most of them have achieved their ambition.

Sam Spiegel

Many directors are just pedestrian workmen who couldn't direct you to a cheap delicatessen.

James Cagney

A director must be a policeman, a midwife, a psycho-analyist, a sycophant and a bastard.

Billy Wilder

If you can drive a car, you can direct a movie.

John Landis

If you give him a good script, actors and technicians, Mickey Mouse could direct a movie.

Nicholas Hytner

To be a director you have to get up very early in the morning. And people keep asking you questions.

Babaloo Mandel

When you're working for a good director, you become his concubine. All that you're seeking is his pleasure.

Donald Sutherland

Directing stars can be nerve-wracking. Woody Allen talks about the pre-21 syndrome. Anybody you saw before the age of 21 on the screen, you'd be a little nervous in directing them. After 21, it's not a problem for some reason.

Martin Scorsese

For me, directing is like having sex: when it's good, it's very good; but when it's bad, it's still good.

Stanley Donen

My idea of a good director is one who puts me center-shot and shines a bright light on me.

John Gielgud

There are no bad actors, only bad directors.

Rex Ingram

When it becomes painful for you not to be a director then you do it.

Orson Welles

I started my career as a drummer; I'm sorry I stopped because it still is the best and the loudest way of calling attention to myself. Being a director comes a close second.

Mel Brooks

Directing is like having a prolonged tantrum. The basic job of a director is to get his own way.

Mike Newell

RELAX!

Otto Preminger to a nervous actor

Because we can't be Stalin, we become movie directors.

Abraham Polonsky

I was fired on the fifth day of shooting Breakin'. The producer, Menahem Golan, told me that I didn't make enough noise to sound like a real director.

David Wheeler

I'm as quiet as a mouse peeing on a blotter.

Norman Z. McLeod

Noël Coward did do some directing and co-directing. It's just not a polite enough profession to suit him, though.

Trevor Howard

One obstacle always stopped me directing films— namely, having to say, "Action!" My instinct would be to say, "Er, I think if everybody's agreeable we might as well sort of start now—that is, if you're ready."

Alan Bennett

My advice to an aspiring director would be, concentrate on the story, leave the details to others—and sit whenever you can.

John Huston

Wear comfortable shoes.

Steven Spielberg

Always remember to fire someone the first day.

Mel Brooks

I have directed 50 pictures, and I'm still crapping in my pants on the first day.

Ernst Lubitsch

All right, kids, it's Rome, it's hot, and here comes
Julius!

Joseph L. Mankiewicz motivating the extras in Julius Caesar

Sparkle, Shirley!

Mrs Temple, her perennial cue to her daughter

Mervyn LeRoy, the director of Quo Vadis, gave me
this gem of advice on how to play the Emperor Nero:
"The way I see Nero, this is the kinda guy who plays
with himself nights."

Peter Ustinov

It doesn't matter what you say, just make something
up.

Woody Allen directing Denholm Elliot

There a thousand ways to point a camera, but really
only one.

Ernst Lubitsch

We paid for the whole actor, Mr Griffith. We expect
to see all of him.

Henry Marvin to D.W. Griffith on seeing the first close-up

The first rule for a young director to follow is not to
direct like Michael Winner. The second and third
rules are the same.

Unnamed director

If you want to become a director, you should sit on top of the camera and pant like a tiger.

Michael Curtiz

I once asked Montgomery Clift, "Would you ever direct yourself?" "Are you kidding?" he said. "As a director, I simply wouldn't put up with all that crap from me."

Myrna Loy

Directing while acting is one less person to argue with.

Roman Polanski

Unlike those directors who say two plus two equals four, Ernst Lubitsch says two plus two—that's it. The audience has to add it up for themselves.

Billy Wilder

The best thing about switching from being an actor to being a director is that you don't have to shave or hold your stomach in anymore.

Dick Powell

Erich von Stroheim was a footage-fetishist.

Irving Thalberg

I remember listening and listening while some guy explained the auteur theory, and all I could think of was this: "What's the punch line?"

William Goldman

People often ask if I'd like to direct, but it would be hard for me to say to someone, "That wasn't very good," and have them say, "Well, what about Popeye?"

Robin Williams

I was driving by Otto Preminger's house last night— or is it a house by Otto Preminger?

Burt Kennedy

A director without a script he can auteur is like a Don Juan without a penis.

Carl Foreman

All good directors take commercial pieces of work for the same reason—fear their careers are in trouble.

William Goldman

The three best directors in Hollywood? John Ford, John Ford, and John Ford.

Orson Welles

Working for Willie Wyler is like getting the works at a Turkish bath. You damn near drown but you come out smelling like a rose.

Charlton Heston

No one else can balance the ups and downs of wistful sentiment and corny humor the way Capra can—but if anyone else should learn to, kill him.

Pauline Kael

I'd rather be Capra than God. If there is a Capra.

Garson Kanin

Like Monet forever painting his lilies, Howard Hawks made only one artwork. Its theme is that men are more expressive rolling a cigarette than saving the world.

David Thomson

I wouldn't want to be a dog, a horse, or a woman around Howard Hawks.

William Faulkner

Mitchell Leisen was a diamond cutter working with lumpy coal.

Andrew Sarris

I'd love to sell out completely. It's just that nobody has been willing to buy.

John Waters

Half-tyrant, half-revolutionary; half-saint, half-satan; half-possible, half-impossible; half-genius, half-Irish.

Frank Capra on John Huston

If you weren't a brilliant writer and a magnificent director, you'd be nothing but a common drunk.

Gregory Ratoff to John Huston

A man of many talents, all of them minor.

Leslie Halliwell on Blake Edwards

Tales of my toughness are exaggerated. I never killed an actor.

John Huston

Sidney Lumet is the only director who could double-park in front of a whore-house. He's that fast.

Paul Newman

Michael Winner's films are atrocious; but they are not the worst thing about him.

Unnamed director

I pride myself on the fact that my work has no socially redeeming value.

John Waters

If you didn't know what industry I worked in it would look like I'm a nut.

Marcus Nispel, director

I wanted to be Frankenstein for a living—it seemed like a good job.

Tim Burton

Robert Altman has most of the qualifications for a major director except the supreme one of having something significant to say.

John Simon

I hope the money men don't find out that I'd pay them to let me do this.

David Lean

I'm over-paid, over-stimulated, over-hyped, over-age, but I am the only person in our business who'll admit it.

Joel Schumacher

Oliver Stone is a heavy-handed propagandist, and the women in his films make Barbie look like Sylvia Plath.

Jane Hamsher

As one of the first women working in a man's world, I was supposed to be aggressive, stony and tough. But maybe I was actually just good.

Gillian Armstrong, director

Ken Russell is an arrogant, self-centered, petulant individual. I don't say this in any demeaning way.

Bob Guccione

While shooting The Cotton Club, Robert Evans behaved like the steward on the *Titanic*, who went into the dining room and said, "Don't worry folks, we're only stopping for more ice."

Richard Sylbert

When he was shooting The Cotton Club I asked Coppola, "Why do you make all this chaos?" And he said, "If nobody knows what's going on, nobody can discuss it with you."

Richard Sylbert

George Lucas has always seemed kind of shy and weirdly modest to me, like Howard Hughes crossed with Mister Rogers. He has always seemed like someone I sould fix up with my dear friend, the tragically single Stacy Schiff, but it would never work, because at some point Stacy would finally crack and ask George if he owns, oh, maybe just one shirt that isn't plaid.

Libby Gelman-Waxner

Sir Stinky Botton, Viscount of Stinkania in the Bottomic Empire.

**Mike Meyers, the name on the back of his director's chair
on the set of Austin Powers: The Spy Who Shagged Me**

James Cameron
The High Priest of Hollywood Bloat.

Richard Corliss

On set, James Cameron behaves like a Renaissance pope.

David Gritten

I don't believe the rumor that during sex, James Cameron's wife is required by a prenuptial agreement to murmur, "You're the king of the world!"

Libby Gelman-Waxner

–Has the success of Titanic changed your husband?

–No, he's always been a jerk.

Reporter and Linda Hamilton, now *ex*-Mrs James Cameron

They'd have to pay me an awful lot of money to work with Jim Cameron again.

Kate Winslet

Jim's a hands-on director and I have the bruises to prove it.

No animals were hurt during the making of this film, but the actors were tossed around like styrofoam cups.

Don't get creative, I hate that.

You either shoot it my way or you do another fucking movie.

Waiting on Lipstick? I say we just tattoo their lips.

Quotes on a crew-member's T-shirt on Titanic

Doing overtime at Dachau.

Crew-member on Titanic

Cecil B. De Mille

Never have I seen a man with so pre-eminent a position splash so fondly about in mediocrity, and, like a child building a sand castle, so serenely convinced that he was producing works of art.

Norman bel Geddes

The B. could stand for many things—Barnum,
Ballyhoo, Box-Office, Baloney, Billion dollars. But,
prosaically enough, it stands for Blount.

Norah Alexander

Give me any two pages of the Bible and I'll give you
a picture.

Cecil B. De Mille

He directed as though chosen by God for this one
task. To suit his role, he wore breeches and high
boots, and carried a revolver. He claimed it was
protection against snakes so often found on his
ranch, but cynics wondered if the serpents in the
picture business caused him to wear such garb at the
studio.

Kevin Brownlow

It did not concern him in the least that in the
opinion of "serious" film makers his works were
considered as artistically significant as Barnum and
Bailey's Circus. He feared only one thing—that an
audience might be bored.

Jessy Lasky Jr

Some day the bastard is going to be crushed
under one of his epics.

W.C. Fields

He wore baldness like an expensive hat, as if it were
out of the question for him to have hair like other men.

Gloria Swanson

I learned an awful lot from him by doing exactly the
opposite.

Howard Hawks

Alfred Hitchcock

Life typecasts us. Look at me. Do you think I would
have chosen to look like this? I would have preferred
to have played a leading man in life. I would have
been Cary Grant.

Alfred Hitchcock

If I made Cinderella people would be looking for the
body in the coach.

Alfred Hitchcock

I have a perfect cure for a sore throat: slit it.

Alfred Hitchcock

I hope to offset any tendency toward the macabre
with humor. As I see it, this is a typically English
form of humor. It's of a piece with such jokes as the
one about the man who was being led to the gallows
to be hanged. He looked at the trap door in the gallows, which was flimsily constructed, and he asked
in some alarm, "I say, is that thing safe?"

Alfred Hitchcock

To me, Psycho is a fun picture. The process through which we take the audience, you see, is rather like taking them through the haunted house at the fairground or the roller-coaster.

Alfred Hitchcock

The comedian Charles Coburn attended the funeral of another comedian Harry Tate. A large assembly of comedians was gathered at the graveside. Old Charles was so ancient that he was retired, and as the coffin was being lowered into the grave, one curious young sprout leaned over and whispered, "How old are you, Charlie?" "89," Coburn said. "Hardly seems worth while you going home," the young 'un said.

Alfred Hitchcock

Hitchcock filmed murder scenes as if they were love scenes and love scenes as if they were murder scenes.

François Truffaut

–Mr Hitchcock, what do you think is my best side?
–My dear, you're sitting on it.

Mary Anderson and Alfred Hitchcock

I've become a body of films, not a man. I am all those films.

Alfred Hitchcock

Stanley Kubrick

He'll be a fine director some day, if he falls flat on his face just once. It might teach him to compromise.

Kirk Douglas

He had a reputation for being difficult. While making Full Metal Jacket, a production assistant was seen repeatedly kicking the set and muttering, "Think of the mortgage, think of the mortgage."

John Baxter

Kubrick's house had the allure of Bluebeard's castle. One did not know, or care to guess how many screenwriters had died and been buried in its recesses.

Frederic Raphael, screenwriter on Eyes Wide Shut

Stanley's good on sound, so are a lot of directors, but Stanley's good on designing a new harness. Stanley's good on the color of the mike, Stanley's good about the merchant he bought the mike from. Stanley's good about the merchant's daughter who needs dental work.

Jack Nicholson

It is said that, like Icarus of Greek myth, D.W. Griffith flew too high and his wings melted. What is the moral of Icarus? "Don't fly too close to the sun?" Or is it, as I choose to believe, "Build better wings."

Stanley Kubrick

Steven Spielberg

I'm surprised for a smart Jew he's as white bread as
he is.

Don Simpson

Spielberg is a genius. I believe that if we can ever
return from some other place and look back a
thousand years from now, he's Shakespeare.

Jeffrey Katzenberg

Disney with technie razzmatazz.

Julie Salamon

It's one of my ambitions to make everyone in an 800-
seat cinema come at the same time.

Steven Spielberg

He's unstoppable. For every film he makes, there are
a thousand more that play in his head. His cranium
houses the world's largest multiplex cinema and it's
open all hours, every day.

Tom Hanks

He admits he hardly ever reads a book. Cartoons
exert a greater influence than literature on his tastes
and assumptions.

David Denby

Walt Disney was my parental conscience, and my
step-parent was the TV set.

Steven Spielberg

Steven Spielberg wanted me for Raiders of the Lost Ark. I explained that I was already shooting with Fassbinder. Spielberg said, "Who's he?"

Giancarlo Giannini

Making E.T. was torture, torture. My pubic hairs turned gray.

Steven Spielberg

Sooner or later, every Life of Spielberg bumps up against the rather alarming fact that he doesn't appear to have lived one.

Tom Shone

I still want to be a director when I grow up.

Steven Spielberg

Quentin Tarantino

The adjective Tarantinoesque never sounds like a flattering thing because it's broken down to black suits, hipper-than-thou dialogue and people talking about TV shows.

Quentin Tarantino

If I hadn't wanted to make movies, I'd have done something that I would have gone to jail for.

Quentin Tarantino

Sylvester Stallone is one of the greatest influences on my career.

Quentin Tarantino

I became an adjective sooner than I thought I was going to.

Quentin Tarantino

I don't make movies that bring people together.

Quentin Tarantino

Billy Wilder

Once in 13 lifetimes do you come across someone like Billy Wilder.

Shirley MacLaine

Long before Billy Wilder was Billy Wilder, he acted as though he was Billy Wilder.

Mrs Billy Wilder

I knew 20 or 30 words of English from American talking pictures. It was too late for me to learn English without an accent. Now, after 50 years, I have a curious accent, which is a mixture of Arnold Schwarzenegger and Archbishop Tutu.

Billy Wilder

Wilder is not a funnyman but a moralist, a recorder of human venality. The Wilder world is one seen at dawn through a hangover, a world of cheap double entendre and stale smoke and drinks in which the ice has melted: the true country of despair.

Joan Didion

Billy Wilder has a mind full of razor blades.

William Holden

Interested persons who open *20th Century Fox's Book of Martyrs* more or less at random are likely to come on text or pictures conveying the nature of my experiences writing with Billy Wilder.

Harry Kurnitz

I remember Billy Wilder opening a bottle of wine. As he strained at the cork, he said, "Forty-five years of masturbation and I still don't have a muscle in my hand."

Frederic Raphael

I have ten commandments. The first nine are "Thou shalt not bore." The tenth is "Thou shalt have the right of final cut."

Billy Wilder

The best director is the one you don't see.

Billy Wilder

If you don't go to people's funerals, they won't come to yours.

Billy Wilder

BEHIND THE
SCREENS

SCREENWRITING

The most important part in film-making is played by the writers. We must do everything in our power to keep them from finding out.

Irving Thalberg

In Hollywood, writers are considered only the first drafts of human beings.

Frank Deford

Did you hear about the starlet so dumb that she slept with the writer?

Producer's joke

Writers in Hollywood are not a tribe of Shelleys in chains, "ruined" by movies. For the most part they are greedy hacks and incompetent thickheads.

Ben Hecht

Writers as a class, I have found to be oversensitive and spiritually undernourished. They have the egotism of actors and rarely the good looks or charm.

Raymond Chandler

Does Hollywood stifle writers? My opinion is that it doesn't stifle enough of them.

Kurt Ambrose

The first draft of anything is shit.

Ernest Hemingway

What's this business about being a writer? It's just
putting one word after another.

Irving Thalberg

Writer's block is a fancy term made up by whiners so
they can have an excuse to drink alcohol.

Steve Martin

Screenwriting is what feminists call "shit-work": if
it's well done, it's ignored. If it's badly done, people
call attention to it.

William Goldman

You never want to see a writer on set. It's like asking
your plumber on honeymoon.

David Mamet

A writer on the set is as much use as a father at the
delivery of a baby.

Luke Morton

On the set, the writer is very much like a hooker
who has been fucked and paid and is there under
sufferance.

Stirling Silliphant

Think of the pitch as the *Reader's Digest* condensed-
novel version of the screenplay.

Lynda Obst

A script-doctor is a man with no original ideas of his
own but specializes instead in ruining the original
ideas of others.

Thomas Beller

Quentin Tarantino, Robert Towne and Steve Zaillian
are the best script-doctors. These guys could punch
up *Hamlet*.

Michael Schiffer

When you are writing a screenplay, one of the things
you are doing, in a sense, is writing a prospectus for
a stock offering.

Howard Rodman

Most of us so-called stars don't have the discipline to
write. Anyway, it's a lot of work for less money.

Richard Gere

The Eleventh Commandment is "Write down."

Ben Hecht

I think nobody writes down. Garbage though they
turn out, Hollywood writers aren't writing down.
That is their best.

Dorothy Parker

They ruin your stories. They massacre your ideas.
They prostitute your art. They trample on your pride.
And what do you get for it? A fortune.

Anonymous screenwriter

–What kind of writing is the most profitable?
–Ransom notes.

Reporter and H.N. Swanson

For $10,000 a week, I'd dramatize the Sears, Roebuck catalogue for a producer who couldn't spell "cat."

Unnamed screenwriter

Anybody can direct a movie, but there are only 11 good writers.

Mel Brooks

Screenwriting is a special kind of job. You need to be a novelist, a playwright and a civil engineer.

Damon Runyon

Being a good screenwriter is no feather bed. You write behind a closed door, and fun is your enemy.

Ben Hecht

The writer's way is rough and lonely, and who would choose it while there are vacancies in more gracious professions, such as, say, cleaning out ferryboats?

Dorothy Parker

The secret of writing is to keep everything moving. Don't let the audience think of the dishes.

Mae West

You couldn't write "fuck" on a dusty venetian blind.

Coral Browne to a screenwriter

Screenplays are tough to write. And tough to read.

Francis Coppola

Raymond Chandler told me to write whatever I wanted to because no one in the front office could read anyway.

Teet Carle

The script is the literary form for a society giving up literacy. People in Hollywood don't read them. Not even the writers read them. They write the scenes out of order and seldom need to scan the whole thing through except to check for page numbers.

David Thomson

It is a distressing experience and a bitter lesson for an author to find that cutting his own work improves it.

Noël Coward

At least 32 writers contributed to the script of The Flintstones. That's more than it took to sign the American Declaration of Independence.

Christopher Tookey

The process of writing a screenplay is like Rodin's description of how to sculpt an elephant: take a large block of stone and remove anything that isn't an elephant.

Marshall Brickman

"Well...how's it coming?" has been the standard greeting to screenwriters throughout the ages, spoken always in a suspicious, accusing tone of voice.

Ken Englund

I orgasmed in the first two months of preparing Raiders of the Lost Ark, then I essentially tore it up and just told the story.

Steven Spielberg

Shit has its own integrity.

Hollywood screenwriters' axiom

A final draft is what you put in the typewriter the night before it's due.

Herman Mankiewicz

Because I've been too fucking busy—and vice versa.

Dorothy Parker explaining why she missed a deadline for delivery of a script

Dahling, they've absolutely ruined your perfectly dreadful play.

Tallulah Bankhead to Tennessee Williams after seeing the film of Orpheus Descending

I agreed to adapt *Pygmalion* on condition that not the least regard be paid to American ideas, except to avoid them as much as possible.

George Bernard Shaw

Selling my book in Hollywood I felt exactly like a merchant selling glass beads to African natives.

Hugh Walpole

Here is a list of my office fees:

For reading a story, with one word comment – $5 a page

For same, without comment – $10 a page

For listening to a story while dozing – $500

For same, wide awake – $1,000

For listening to a story described jovially as "just a springboard" – $10,000

For reading stories, plays of scripts written by actors or actresses to star themselves – $25.000

For looking at talented children – $500

For talking to same – $50,000

For meeting "new faces," male – $100

For same, female – $1

For same, female, door closed – No charge

In cases of friends or warm acquaintances acquired the night before in saloons, the fees are double.

Nunnally Johnson, letter to Norman Corwin

The Hollywood film version of my play, Design For Living, retained only one line intact: "Kippers on toast."

Noël Coward

Seeing your book turned into a movie is like
watching your children get raped by Cossacks.

Kathy Lette

Giving your book to Hollywood is like pimping your
daughter.

Tom Clancy

Hollywood is the place where they take an author's
steak tartare and make cheeseburger out of it.

Fletcher Knebel

In Hollywood we acquire the finest novels in order to
smell the leather bindings.

Ernst Lubitsch

One time on the set of The Moonshine Wars, the
actor Patrick McGoohan came up to me and said,
"What's it like to stand there and hear your lines all
fucked up?"

Elmore Leonard

They have done nothing to my books. They are right
over there on the shelf exactly as I wrote them.

James M. Cain

They paid vast sums of money and never made the
film, which is the best of both worlds.

P.D. James on her novel, *Innocent Blood*

Boy, I've an idea. Let's fill the screen with tits.

Hunt Stromberg

No story ever looks as bad as the story you've just bought; no story ever looks as good as the story the other fellow just bought.

Irving Thalberg

A book is something they make a movie out of.

Leonard Louis Levenson

Never judge a book by a motion picture with the same title.

LA Times

The picture occupied four years of my life, writing and rewriting, over 300 drafts in all.

Ed Naha on Honey, I Shrunk the Kids

So many people read the screenplay for Desperately Seeking Susan that we figured if the film ever got made, there'd be no one left to see it.

Midge Sandford

"Change this scene!" Harry Cohn railed. I protested, "Why? Give me one reason." Cohn said, "The reason is: I am the president of Columbia Pictures."

Rouben Mamoulian

Alexander Woollcott did not approve of our adaptation of *Wuthering Heights*. He said, "You vandals! You've raped Emily Brontë!" To which Charlie MacArthur replied, "She's been waiting for it for years."

Ben Hecht

A producer pointed out to one of his writers, in the heat of an argument, that he couldn't possibly be wrong because he was worth 2 million dollars.

George Oppenheimer

If you were forced to read the book in high school, you'll probably hate the movie, too.

Andy Ihnatko

There is a simple law governing the dramatization of novels: if it is worth doing, it can't be done. If it can be done, it isn't worth it.

John Simon

I have tried to remain faithful to the book, which is more than I did with my wife.

Woody Allen

I wrote the script for Rocky in 3 days. I'm astounded by people who take 18 years to write something. That's how long it took that guy to write *Madame Bovary*. And did that ever make the best-seller list?

Sylvester Stallone

Not many executives actually read books in Hollyood. Their lips get tired after ten pages.

Richard Sylbert

I would rather take a 50-mile hike than crawl through a book.

Jack L. Warner

To bring a sense of perfection to Hollywood is to go bagging tigers with a fly swatter.

Ben Hecht

If you want to say something as a writer, screen-writing must be the least efficient means of doing so. You're really better off putting a message in a bottle.

David Pirie

Larry, the producer, was full of suggestions for the script...change this scene, add that scene, change this character, add that character... "Larry," I said, "where were you when the page was blank?"

Fred Allen

—I thought I asked you to alter the script.
—I did.
—All you did was change the words.

Sam Goldwyn and screenwriter

Nijinski was the greatest dancer ever...ended up in a French nuthouse, thinking he was a horse, but don't worry, there's a happy ending. In the final scene, he wins the Kentucky Derby.

Billy Wilder pitching a movie to Louis B. Mayer

In the U.S. you can fall back on stars so scripts don't have to be that good. No other country in the world has that backstop.

John Manulis, Goldwyn Entertainment executive, 1997

Hollywood should jettison the notion of unrealistic happy endings. After all, Rick never got on the plane with Elsa; Zhivago died before he was reunited with Lara; and Wile E. Coyote never caught the Road Runner.

Boyd Farrow

The executives who read the script say: "Well, the main character is not very likeable." So without changing what the main character says or does, when I introduce them, I write, Betty a very likeable person, then they go, "Oh, these changes are wonderful! She really comes alive!" I do that all the time.

Don Roos

I have seen your film Battleship Potemkin and admired it very much. What we should like would be for you to do something of the same kind, but rather cheaper, for Ronald Colman.

Sam Goldwyn to Sergei Eisenstein

Broken Blossoms isn't commercial. Everyone in it dies.

Adolph Zukor

Raymond Chandler could write a beautiful sentence: "There is nothing as empty as an empty swimming pool." But he could not construct a good plot.

Billy Wilder

Louis B. Mayer wanted all his movies to fade out
with bells ringing, rose petals softening the path of
lovers until the camera gazed mistily on a handsome
and triumphant groom embracing a beautiful
blushing bride in the inevitable happy ending.

Arthur Marx

While shooting The Big Sleep we were having
trouble figuring out all the twists in the plot. I
cabled Raymond Chandler and asked him who killed
General Sternwood's chauffeur in the original story.
Chandler sent a wire back saying, NO IDEA.

Howard Hawks

If my books had been any worse I should not have
been invited to Hollywood; if they had been any
better I should not have come.

Raymond Chandler

What I have crossed out I didn't like. What I haven't
crossed out I am dissatisfied with.

Cecil B. De Mille turning down a script

We'd like you to pump up the final part of Ben Hur.
We find there is a sort of anti-climax after the
Crucifixion.

Sam Zimbalist to Graham Greene

There's an awful lot of Greeks in it.

Harry Cohn turning down an adaptation of *The Iliad*

There are three rules to screenwriting.
Unfortunately, no one knows what they are.

Brad Lucas

Nobody wants to see a movie about a little brown man in a loincloth.

Unnamed studio executive turning down Gandhi

Does she have to pray so much?

Senior studio executive to Ronald Maxwell
about his script, Joan of Arc

I suggested to the producer that the story would work better if it was set in 1820. "1820?" he said, "When was that?"

Ed Hartman

A pseudosophisticated producer looked at a script and said, "It lacks—I don't quite know how to say it in English—effervescence." The same producer objected to the backgound music in a Tarzan film because it shattered the reality.

George Oppenheimer

Who would really want to write for porno movies? I mean, how many ways are there to say "big tits?"

Max Rainer

You can type this shit, George, but you sure can't say it.

Harrison Ford to George Lucas, writer of Star Wars

My lines in Tarzan, the Ape Man, read like a back-
ward two-year-old talking to his nurse: "Tarzan,
Jane, hurt me, boy, love it, Jane."

Johnny Weissmuller

John Frankenheimer called up and said, "Our
Japanese actor, Toshiro, is a little shaky with his Rs
and Ls. Could we get rid of the Rs and Ls?" So I went
through his dialogue taking out as many words
beginning with R and L as I could—which is an
interesting way to write a screenplay.

John Sayles

This is a terrific script. It just needs a complete
rewrite.

Peter Bogdanovich to Alvin Sargent, writer of Paper Moon

At UCS, I took Latin and Romance Languages, and
mathematics. And when I started in movies, they had
to teach me to say "ain't."

John Wayne

The big films today are like cartoon strips, and the
dialogue is the kind that you read in their balloons.

Joseph L. Mankiewicz, 1986

As for Samuel Beckett, I took one look at his script
and asked him if he ate Welsh rarebit before he went
to bed at night.

Buster Keaton

Hell, I ain't paid to make good lines sound good, I'm paid to make bad lines sound good.

Walter Huston

The best short scene I ever wrote, by my judgement, was one in which a girl said "uh-huh" three times with different intonations, and that's all there was to it.

Raymond Chandler

—Make him sound more like a Pharoah.
—I don't know how a Pharoah talks.

**Howard Hawks and William Faulkner on
Land of the Pharoahs**

John Barrymore had a perfect memory and could recite all the soliloquies from *Hamlet*, but he still insisted on using idiot cards in his movies. He said, "Why should I fill my mind with this shit just to forget it tomorrow morning?"

Mitchell Leisen

I don't know what the script's about, but it reminds me of the fear I get now and again of having to drink a glass of water without the glass.

Herman Mankiewicz

Bury it in a drawer with a lily on top.

Noël Coward, advice about a script

Tom Stoppard, Joe Orton and Joseph Heller all had a crack at the script of Yellow Submarine, but Brian Epstein selected a version by Erich Segal mainly because he liked the color of the folder it was in.

Mark Steyn

I wrote Sister Act as a vehicle for Bette Midler. Disney watered it down so much for Whoopi Goldberg that it no longer felt like my work. I agreed on a pseudonym, Joseph Howard, for the screen-credit after my first choice, "Screenplay by Goofy" was turned down.

Paul Rudnick (a.k.a. Libby Gelman-Waxner)

—I should put more fire in my script, right?
—No. Vice versa.

Screenwriter and John Huston

It has no story, no characterization, no excitement, but it is some of the finest typing I have ever seen.

Norman Krasna

Movie writing is not easier than good writing. It's just as hard to make a toilet seat as it is a castle window. But the view is different.

Ben Hecht

Ben Hecht made himself into a hack, a hack of genius.

Hugh Gray

Good original screenplays are almost as rare in Hollywood as virgins.

Raymond Chandler

The secret of being a successful screenwriter is you have to write very, very badly, but you also have to write as well as you possibly can.

Christopher Hampton

A good script is a script to which Robert Redford has committed himself. A bad script is a script Robert Redford has turned down. A script that "needs work" is a script about which Robert Redford has yet to make up his mind.

Pauline Kael

—What do you look for in a script?
—Days off.

Interviewer and Robert Mitchum

F. Scott Fitzgerald made me think of a great sculptor who is hired to do a plumbing job. He did not know how to connect the fucking pipes so the water would flow.

Billy Wilder

In the throes of composition George S. Kaufman seems to crawl up the walls of the apartment in the manner of the late Count Dracula.

Alexander Woollcott

Listening to Alexander Woollcott is like being hit with a cream puff; you are uninjured but rather sickened.

Robert Forsythe

Dorothy Parker called her canary "Onan" because of his habit of spilling his seed on the ground.

Robert Benchley

Raymond Chandler looked rather like a boffin in an Ealing comedy.

J.B. Priestley

I.A.L. Diamond was the world's greatest collaborator, with the possible exception of Quisling.

Billy Wilder

I knew William Faulkner well. He was a great friend of mine. Well, much as you could be a friend of his, unless you were a 14-year-old nymphet.

Truman Capote

—Do you write Mr Faulkner?
—Yes, Mr Gable. What do you do?

William Faulkner and Clark Gable

The surest way to make money in Hollywood, judging by the shopfronts out there, is to set up a photocopy shop Xeroxing everyone's scripts.

Joe Joseph

CASTING

Casting is deciding which of two faces the public is least tired of.

Marcia Lynch

They made the decision on the lead in Flashdance by taking tapes of all the auditioning actresses into a room with a bunch of guys and asking, "Who would you want to fuck?" I was astounded by that.

Jennifer Beals

If Tom Cruise comes in and says he wants to play Princess Di in a musical of her life, we'd do it, it's the way the business works.

Unnamed producer

What makes somebody hot? Somebody else thinking someone's hot, makes somebody hot. It's that simple.

Jeremy Zimmer

I direct as little as possible. I relieve myself of the ardors of direction simply by casting it right.

John Huston

There are three rules of picture-making: casting, casting, casting. Look at George Hamilton—how many bombs has he been in in his life? Then he played a funny vampire—a $100 million.

Joel Silver

You begin by casting Tom Cruise, Julia Roberts and Tom Hanks, but by the time shooting starts, you're just grateful if your actors aren't albinos.

Frank Zwemmer

Keanu Reeves? I couldn't cast someone who sounds like a small Polynesian island.

Terence Davies

Always cast against the part and it won't be boring.

David Lean

I was quite discomknockerated when Kenneth Branagh invited me to take the part of Yorick in the great saga of *Hamlet*.

Ken Dodd

I was concerned about being in drag for Dressed To Kill. I thought, suppose I like it?

Michael Caine

Charles Laughton called me up: "I've a book here about a thoroughly unredeemable shit." And I said: "Present!"

Robert Mitchum accepting the role of the Preacher in The Night of the Hunter

I can't play a loser. I don't look like one.

Rock Hudson

No mammas, no murderesses.

Greta Garbo on choosing her roles

I do the kinds of roles I'd like to see if I were still
digging swimming pools and wanted to escape my
problems.

Clint Eastwood

I always choose my roles on the basis of the location
of the shoot.

Michael Caine

Those little virgins, after five minutes you got so sick
of playing them—to make them interesting was hard
work.

Lillian Gish

What kinda whore am I this time?

Jean Harlow to her agent

If the Martians landed and did nothing but go to
the movies this year, they would come to the fair
conclusion that the chief occupation of women on
earth is hooking.

Meryl Streep, 1990

Unless she's a whore, she's a bore.

Billy Wilder on roles for women in movies

I made my debut as Freak #1 in Michael Winner's
Death Wish. I had to attack Charles Bronson's wife
and daughter in the opening scene. At my audition,
Winner threw a chair at me and said, "Rape that!"

Jeff Goldblum

No one can deny that women get a pretty rough deal in the movies. Roles for women hit rock bottom a few years ago with a picture about a beautiful young woman who had her limbs removed and was trapped, half-naked in a world deprived of oxygen and sunlight. But enough about The Little Mermaid.

Boyd Farrow

In most action movies, women are in the way.

Arnold Schwarzenegger

The only time I ever use women in films, they're either naked or dead.

Joel Silver

After The Wizard of Oz I was typecast as a lion, and there aren't all that many parts for lions.

Bert Lahr

I'm typecast anyway—as me.

Roger Moore

I was up for a great part but they told me: "Sorry, you're the best actor but this role calls for a guy-next-door type. You don't look like you've ever lived next door to anyone."

Donald Sutherland

I've done it all. I've played everything but a harp.

Lionel Barrymore, proposed epitaph

Scarlett O'Hara is going to be a thankless and difficult role. The part I'd like to play is Rhett Butler.

Norma Shearer

Margaret Mitchell's only casting suggestion for Gone With the Wind was for her favorite star to play Rhett: Groucho Marx.

George Cukor

Why should I complain about making $7,000 a week playing a maid? If I didn't, I'd be making $7 a week being one.

Hattie McDaniel

We shot Love and Death in the Balkans using contingents of the Red Army. They were thrilled to be in a movie because their life was so boring...just occupying Hungary.

Woody Allen

They got a lot of the extras for One Flew Over the Cuckoo's Nest through an ad in the local paper that said: Do you have a face that scares timberwolves?

Jack Nicholson

—Who do I have to screw to get out of this picture?
—The same person you screwed to get into it.

Hollywood joke

It's not true about the casting couch. You can only fuck your way to the middle.

Sharon Stone

Disney, of course, has the best casting. It he doesn't like an actor, he just tears him up.

Alfred Hitchcock

MUSIC

The movies should have married music instead of words.

Lillian Gish

They don't want films in Hollywood. What they want is a soundtrack they can sell.

Peter Mullan, 1998

Movie music is like a coat of wax on a beautiful car.

Don Simpson

Don Simpson makes soundtracks in search of movies.

Julia Phillips

Movie music is noise, even more painful than my sciatica.

Sir Thomas Beecham

Frankly, Seth, the movie is an hour too long, the performances stink, and the story falls apart five minutes after the front credits. So we have no choice. We have to redo the music.

Alan Parker, cartoon caption

102

Hitchcock only finished a picture 60 per cent. I have to finish it off for him.

Bernard Hermann, composer

Bernie cut a faintly shambolic figure. If he had become an angel, he would have had soup stains on his robe after the first lunch.

Friend of Bernard Hermann

If you notice the music in a film, the composer isn't doing his job.

Simon Boswell, composer

What makes a great film score is a great film.

Lewis Gilbert

Film music should have the same relationship to the film drama that somebody's piano playing in my living room has to the book I am reading.

Igor Stravinsky

The inspiration for the new Star Wars music came to me as I was sitting on the toilet, watching *General Hospital*. All of a sudden, the water gushed and brought together a syncopated harmony perfect for the theme of the boy who will one day become Darth Vader.

John Williams

I hate music, especially when it's played.

Jimmy Durante

I was worried the concerto played over the climactic scenes in E.T. was just too lush. I asked Spielberg if he really thought we'd get away with it. "Steven, it's shameless," I said. "John," he replied, "movies are shameless."

John Williams

The one thing I can say about Tim Roth's piano-playing in The Legend of the Pianist on the Ocean is that he has excellent posture.

Ennio Morricone

I am leaving 20th Century Fox because I do not want to spend the rest of my life manufacturing music to be played while Debbie Reynolds speaks.

André Previn

VOICES

My daughter's got a voice like chalk on a black-board.

Judy Garland on Liza Minnelli

Tarzan's distinctive ape-man cry was created for Weissmuller by blending a whole series of unconnected sounds—a camel's bleat, a hyena's yowl played backwards, a pluck of a violin string, a soprano's high C, and Weissmuller's bellowing at the top of his lungs.

Ronald Bergan

Clint Eastwood developed his way of talking by studying the breathy speech pattern of Marilyn Monroe.

Sondra Locke

I would rather listen to Bloch's String Quartet played in a goods-yard, with shunting operations in full swing and all the Jews trying to get into or out of Palestine (I never know which) wailing up against the walls—there is no noise known to me, including the road drill, and the later compositions of Bela Bartok, that I execrate so deeply as the squawking of that abominable fowl.

James Agate on Donald Duck

Rosie Perez's voice would drive me back to heroin.

Charlie Sheen

My voice is a cross between Donald Duck and a Stradivarius.

Katharine Hepburn

That wonderful voice of hers—strange, fey, mysterious, like a voice singing in the snow.

Louise Brooks on Margaret Sullavan

With its unaccustomed rhythm and sing-song cadence that develops into a flat drawl ending in a childlike query, it has the quality of heartbreak.

Cecil Beaton on Audrey Hepburn

Purred elegance.

Peter Bogdanovich on Audrey Hepburn

Jimmy Stewarts sang in Born To Dance. It was a high, higher voice, close to the sound range that only bats and women in love can hear.

David Thomson

Maurice Chevalier put a song over as if he were humming to himself for his own pleasure with a rhythm and sureness of touch that took my breath away.

Mistinguette

For Everyone Says I Love You, only Drew Barrymore's singing voice was dubbed. It was outside the limits of human tolerance.

Woody Allen

Drew Barrymore sings so badly, deaf people refuse to watch her lips move.

Woody Allen

Accents? I can do Irish, Welsh, Manchester, Liverpool, Birmingham, cockney and New York Jewish lesbian.

Julie Walters

SET DESIGN

I've been to Paris, France, and I've been to Paris, Paramount. I think I prefer Paris, Paramount.

Ernst Lubitsch

We travelled the length and breadth of Scotland
scouting locations for Brigadoon but we found
nothing that resembled Scotland, so we constructed
the Highlands in the studio.

Arthur Freed

When I arrived for the filming of Ben Hur, all the
sets had been built, including Charlton Heston.

Gore Vidal

In Batman, I wanted Gotham City to look like New
York without planning permission for 300 years.

Anton Furst, set designer

In A Midsummer Night's Dream, the sylvan sets,
with their plastic fruit and Victorian sprites, look
like they were designed by the people who did the
Posh-Becks wedding.

Edward Porter

There'll always be an England—even if it's in
Hollywood.

Bob Hope

If the scripts were as great as the sets, what a town
Hollywood would be.

Somerset Maugham

AGENTS

In Hollywood nothing is certain but death, and taxes, and agents.

Leo Rosten

An agent is a a guy who's sore because an actor gets 90% of what he makes.

Alva Johnson

Talent is rare, and the talent to handle talent is very rare, and the talent to handle your own talent is almost non-existent.

Jerry Wald

You can tell real talent at once. There is an originality, a vitality. Real talent should surprise you. No, it should alarm you.

Peggy Ramsay, agent

I don't know anything about movies. In my line you don't have to.

Alan Berg, agent

An agent has to know how to say, "Fuck you" with style.

Carl Hoffman

Schmoozing is important. It is harder for someone to screw you if they've had dinner at your house.

Sue Mengers, agent

Our relationship with agents can be summed up in a sentence: We pray they don't kill us in our sleep.

Howard Rodman, screenwriter

To be dependent on an agent is like entrusting your most precious future to your mother-in-law or your bookmaker.

John Osborne

Little by little, the pimps have taken over the world. They don't do anything, they don't make anything— they just stand there and take their cut.

Jean Giraudoux

Michael Ovitz is a combination of a barracuda and Mother Teresa.

Paul Newman

Mike Ovitz is even colder than his air-conditioned office.

Julia Phillips

I worship the ground my agent is buried in.

Unnamed actor

Jeff Berg is a very good agent. That's a terrible thing to say about someone in their 20s.

Julia Phillips

If you cross Ray Stark, you'd better make sure he's dead first.

Unnamed actor

UP IN LIGHTS

ACTORS & ACTING

I always knew that if all else failed I could become an actor—and all else failed.

David Niven

An actor is not quite a human being—but then, who is?

George Sanders

There are two types: toupée actors and non-toupée actors.

Donald Pleasance

Only difference between me and other actors is I've spent more time in jail.

Robert Mitchum

—Why did you want to become an actor?
—Because I thought I'd meet a lot of queers.

Reporter and Ian McKellen

My mother was against me being an actress—until I introduced her to Frank Sinatra.

Angie Dickinson

She goes, "I'm an actress." I go, "Sure, which restaurant?"

Sandra Bernhard

It's no job for a grown man.

Laurence Olivier

An actress I met assured me her real ambition was to be a waitress at a coffeehouse.

Woody Allen

An actress is someone with no ability who sits around waiting to go on alimony.

Jackie Stallone

I'm an actor. An actress is someone who wears boa feathers.

Sigourney Weaver

I'm no actor, and I have 64 pictures to prove it.

Victor Mature

There are five stages in the life of an actor: Who's Mary Astor? Get me Mary Astor. Get me a Mary Astor type. Get me a young Mary Astor. Who's Mary Astor?

Mary Astor

Don't ever forget what I'm going to tell you. Actors are crap.

John Huston

It sure beats working.

Robert Mitchum

The only good thing about acting in movies is that there's no heavy lifting.

Cary Grant

I learned two things at drama school: first, that I couldn't act; second, that it didn't matter.

Wilfred Hyde-White

Acting is largely a matter of farting about in disguises.

Peter O'Toole

I flunked my screen test at 20th Century Fox. The studio thought my test was so bad that they saved it to use as an example of bad acting.

Rock Hudson

Acting is simple. You knock on the door. A guy says, "Open the door, come in." If you open the door and come in, you're a good actor.

George Burns

Acting is not the things you say, it's the things you don't say.

Judi Dench

To become a good actor, you have to keep watching, and if you see nothing worth copying, you'll see something to avoid.

Al Pacino

The whole thing is to keep working, and pretty soon they'll think you're good.

Jack Nicholson

I know nothing about acting so I have one rule—
trust the director and give him heart and soul.
And nothing else.

Ava Gardner

The actor and the streetwalker...the two oldest
professions in the world - ruined by amateurs.

Alexander Woollcott

I'm a pro: I'm never late. I try to control flatulence.

Donald Sutherland

—What acting advice can you give me?
—Get a good tan.

William Holden and Cary Grant

Arrive sober, on time and know all the jokes.

David Niven

Know your lines and don't bump into the furniture.

Spencer Tracy

First wipe your nose and check your flies.

Alec Guinness

Talk low, talk slow, and don't talk too fucking much.

John Wayne

My acting range? Left eyebrow raised, right eyebrow
raised.

Roger Moore

Listen, I got three expressions: looking left, looking right and looking straight ahead.

Robert Mitchum

I do two kinds of acting: loud and soft.

Bing Crosby

Marion Davies has two expressions: joy and indigestion.

Dorothy Parker

Clint Eastwood has two expressions on camera: sullen and angry. Off camera, he has one: very, very rich.

Don Siegel

Kenneth Tynan said I had only two gestures: left hand up, and right hand down. What did he want me to do, bring out my prick?

John Gielgud

If I have occasionally given brilliant performances on the screen, this was entirely due to circumstances beyond my control.

George Sanders

I was once refused membership of a golf club because club rules forbade actors from joining. I sent them the reviews I got for my Bond films and was immediately allowed to join.

Roger Moore

116

If I kept all my bad notices, I'd need two houses.

Roger Moore

In Dragonheart, instead of a dragon, I acted with a tennis ball on a stick. I've worked with some actors who've given me less.

Dennis Quaid

The kids keep telling me I should try this new "Method acting" but I'm too old, I'm too tired and I'm too talented to care.

Spencer Tracy

I'm the thug in The Avengers. I just stare at people and hit them. Oh, and I chew gum—that was my Method touch.

Eddie Izzard

Dear boy, why don't you just act?

Laurence Olivier to Dustin Hoffman

If you must have motivation, think of your pay packet on Friday.

Noël Coward

You can learn more by watching Cary Grant drink a cup of coffee than by spending six months with a Method actor.

Tony Curtis

If it works, that's The Method.

Jack Nicholson

I don't go for this Method-acting stuff. I'm never going to be a Meryl Streep. But then, she'll never be a Dolly Parton either.

Dolly Parton

I went to hear a talk about "The Method." Miss Paula Strasberg went off into a long dissertation on the art of acting, most of which was pretentious balls.

Noël Coward

—I've been studying Stanislavski.
—Stan who?

Stephen Fry and Hugh Laurie

Method actors give you a photograph. Real actors give you an oil painting.

Charles Laughton

Method acting? There are quite a few methods. Mine involves a lot of talent, a glass and some cracked ice.

John Barrymore

What I am trying to express, with just my back as I walk away, is a warning against nuclear destruction.

Kenpachiro Satsuma, the actor in
the monster suit in Godzilla

You're acting! Don't act! I don't act, that's why I'm a star.

Errol Flynn

There's a very fine line between underacting and not acting at all. And not acting is what a lot of actors are guilty of. It amazes me how some of these little numbers with dreamy looks and a dead pan are getting away with it. I'd hate to see them on stage with a dog act.

Joan Blondell

–Thank goodness I don't have to act with you any more.

–I didn't know you ever had, darling.

Katharine Hepburn and John Barrymore
after A Bill of Divorcement

If you haven't complete rapport with the actress with whom you are acting it is like being thrust into the middle of a particularly edgy bullfight.

Peter Ustinov

Acting is like masturbation—one either does it or one doesn't, but one never talks about it.

Eric Portman

Don't just do something. Stand there.

Clint Eastwood

STARS

I like Demi Moore. But that's because I have no taste.

Joe Queenan

Demi Moore is the Arnold Schwarzenegger of women.

Candace Bushnell

Gwyneth Paltrow is quite pretty in a British, horsey sort of way.

Julia Roberts

Minnie Driver is the Amanda de Cadenet who made it.

Courtney Love

Uma Thurman looks like a giraffe that has wandered off the Nature Reserve and panicked.

Guardian

Gillian Anderson looks like a supply teacher.

David Baddiel

Richard E. Grant looks rather like one of those balloons you get from the National Gallery of Munch's The Scream, after it's burst.

Deborah Ross

Daniel Day-Lewis is the child of former Poet Laureate Cecil Day-Lewis and not, as some Americans assume, Doris Day's son by Jerry Lewis.

Mark Steyn

Kenneth Branagh has a lot of the qualities the British hate in Americans—naked ambition, relentless chirpiness, optimism.

Hollywood studio executive

I pretty much try to stay in a constant state of confusion just because of the expression it leaves on my face.

Johnny Depp

Clint Eastwood is looking increasingly like an Easter Island statue.

Time Out

–How would you define the quintessential Clint Eastwood picture?
–To me, a Clint Eastwood picture is one that I'm in.

Interviewer and Clint Eastwood

It is impossible to make too many nasty remarks about short, bad actors related to Martin Sheen.

Joe Queenan

Michael Caine is an over-fat, flatulent 62-year-old windbag, a master of inconsequence, now masquerading as a guru, passing off his vast limitations as pious virtues.

Richard Harris

Richard Harris is something of a fuck-up, no question.

Charlton Heston

I'd wring your neck, if you had one.

Noël Coward to Claudette Colbert

My hair makes me look like a Talmudic scholar.

Tom Hanks

You don't hear about Tom Hanks running around nights. You don't hear about Tom Hanks stealing. You don't read about Tom Hanks in *The National Enquirer*. That's what I like about Tom. He never gets caught.

Jack Nicholson

My grandmother was utterly convinced I'd wind up as the Archbishop of Canterbury. And, to be honest, I've never entirely ruled it out.

Hugh Grant

Raquel Welch is one of the few actresses in Hollywood history who looks more animated in still photographs than she does on the screen.

Michael Medved

Mercedes Ruel is a brassy brunette with a body worth swimming a moat for.

Anon

I got happy every morning when I saw Glenda Jackson. She always looked ready for trouble.

Walter Matthau

Spencer Tracy's face was craggy, freckled and rough-hewn. It was tough and sturdy and sunburned and later seamed with a network of wrinkles. Someone once said the lines would hold two days of rain. He himself said his face reminded him of a beat-up barn door.

David Zinman

–Aren't you tired of always playing Spencer Tracy?

–What I am supposed to do, play Humphrey Bogart?

Interviewer and Spencer Tracy

Spencer Tracy didn't act, he just behaved.

Humphrey Bogart

Barbara Stanwyck is my favorite. My God, I could just sit and dream of being married to her, having a little cottage out in the hills, vines around the door. I'd come home from the office tired and weary, and I'd be met by Barbara, walking through the door holding an apple pie she had cooked herself. And wearing no underwear.

Billy Wilder

Billy Connolly's habitual expression is like a cat with its tail beneath a rocking chair.

Anon

Melanie Griffith is very sweet but dumb–the lights are on but the dogs aren't barking.

Joan Rivers

Griffith, Melanie: ability to turn a man's saliva into gravy; addresses issue of fist-fucking; Betsy Wetsy voice of; Chatty Cathy voice of; frustrated attempts to study philosophy at the Sorbonne; inexplicable career of; large butt of.

> Joe Queenan, index entry in his book, *If You're Talking to Me, Your Career Must Be in Trouble*

Kim Basinger is a blow-up doll come to life: leggy legs, stick-on breasts, pumped-up lips—like a custom-built woman who's been ordered à la carte.

Mark Steyn

John Wayne is a son of bitch, but he's the sort of son of a bitch I like.

Howard Hawks

Julie Andrews has that wonderful British strength that makes you wonder why they lost India.

Moss Hart

Julie Andrews has lilacs for pubic hairs.

Blake Edwards, her husband

One wishes Julie Andrews didn't always give the impression that she had just left her horse in the hallway.

Michael Billington

A face unclouded by thought.

Lillian Hellman on Norma Shearer

In Raiders of the Lost Ark, I did the scenes where I'm dragged behind the truck myself. I figured if it really was dangerous, they would have filmed more of the movie first.

Harrison Ford

I don't sing, tap dance, juggle, or say "Sir."

Bill Cosby

Robert Redford has turned almost alarmingly blond
—he's gone past platinum, he must be plutonium; his
hair is coordinated with his teeth.

Pauline Kael

Nowadays, Robert Redford's skin looks like a child's
sandpit after heavy rain.

Lynn Barber

Nobody said we had to be bright. It's not in the
contract.

Tim Roth

I don't need bodyguards. I'm from the South Bronx.

Al Pacino

I told Robert De Niro he was a class-A bastard. He
said, "I don't mind being a bastard, as long as I'm an
interesting bastard."

Liza Minnelli

Robert De Niro's our greatest actor. So acting with
him became the biggest challenge of my career.
When you start to work, it's like the first time you
shower in gym class together.

Billy Crystal on Analyze This

Robert De Niro is a very intense actor. He doesn't
play joy well.

Neil Simon

It's hard to recall what Ellen Burstyn looks like in between her movies.

David Denby

Alec Guinness looks unmemorable. Were he to commit a murder, I have no doubt that the number of false arrests following the circulation of his description would break all records.

Kenneth Tynan

I really don't know who I am. Quite possibly, I do not exist at all.

Alec Guinness

There used to be a me, but I had it surgically removed.

Peter Sellers

What do you mean, heart attack? You've got to have a heart before you can have an attack.

Billy Wilder on Peter Sellers

I have been known to cause diabetes in some people.

Meg Ryan

My movies are the kind they show in prison and on airplanes because nobody can leave.

Burt Reynolds

Poor Ingrid—speaks five languages and can't act in any of them.

John Gielgud on Ingrid Bergman

Montgomery Clift was the most sensitive man I've ever known. If somebody kicked a dog a mile away he'd feel it.

Edward Dmytryk

Ingrid Bergman had a superabundance of all the virtues of the Swedes—innocence, romanticism and emotional recklessness—and all their faults—innocence, romanticism and emotional recklessness.

Sam White

When Ingrid Bergman walks on screen and says, "Hello" people ask, "Who wrote that wonderful line of dialogue?"

Leo McCarey

Maggie Smith acts like Quentin Crisp in drag.

James Coco

Margaret Rutherford's appearance suggests an overstuffed electric chair. Her writhing stare could reduce a rabid dog to foaming jelly.

Time magazine

The unique thing about Margaret Rutherford is that she can act with her chin alone. Among its many moods I especially cherish the chin commanding, the chin in doubt, the chin at bay.

Kenneth Tynan

A swaggering, tough little slut.

> Louise Brooks on Shirley Temple, aged 11

Infancy with Shirley Temple is a disguise, her appeal is more secret and more adult... She is a complete totsy. Watch the way she measures a man with agile studio eyes, with dimpled depravity.

> Graham Greene, 1937

In one scene in Jinxed I had to hit Bette Midler in the face, and I thought, we could save some money on sound effects here.

> Ken Wahl

Isn't it wonderful you've had such a great career when you had no right to have a career at all?

> Katharine Hepburn to Dorothy Arzner

If that child had been born in the Middle Ages, she'd have been burned as a witch.

> Lionel Barrymore on Margaret O'Brien

Kevin Costner is like Oakland: there is no there there.

> Marcello Mastroianni

I love Mickey Mouse more than any woman I've ever known.

> Walt Disney

Who'd pay to see a drawing of a fairy princess when you can watch Joan Crawford's boobs for the same price?

> Louis B. Mayer on Snow White and the Seven Dwarfs

Walt Disney said, "Shit," and the rest of the words, and he'd talk about turds for thirty minutes without pausing for breath. At the bottom line, he was a down-to-earth farmer's son who just happened to be a genius.

Ward Kimball

I could never convince the financiers that Disneyland was feasible because dreams offer too little collateral.

Walt Disney

Euro Disneyland is a cultural Chernobyl.

Arlene Mnouchkine

My dad doesn't draw Bugs Bunny. He draws pictures of Bugs Bunny.

5-year-old son of Chuck Jones, animator

I called her Sorrows of the River.

George Sanders on Dolores Del Rio

Kirk Douglas would be the first man to tell you he's a difficult man. I would be the second.

Burt Lancaster

I suppose Kirk Douglas looks all right if your tastes happen to run to septuagenarians with blow-waves and funny stretch-marks round the ears.

Lynn Barber

To read Shirley MacLaine's autobiography is to encounter one of the most inflated airheads ever to break free of her moorings.

John Preston

The oars aren't touching the water these days.

Dean Martin on Shirley MacLaine

It's a damn good thing he never co-starred with Lassie.

Shirley MacLaine on Warren Beatty

Think what Warren Beatty could have achieved if he'd been celibate.

Shirley MacLaine

I read that you live like a monk, except for the celibacy part.

Oprah Winfrey to Richard Gere

Chuck Norris is an actor whose lack of expression is so profound that it could be mistaken for icily controlled technique.

Nicholas Lezard

Laurence Olivier will spend thirty seconds sizing you up, decide what kind of person you want him to be, and then he will turn into that person.

Kenneth Tynan

At his worst, Laurence Olivier could have acted the parts more ably than they are usually lived.

Anon

Laurence Olivier is the most overrated actor on earth.
Take away the wives and the looks, and you have
John Gielgud.

Oscar Levant

I may not be as good as Olivier but I'm taller than he
is.

Roger Moore

Judy Garland, already a star at 12, was a compulsive
weeper. She was such a good actress that listeners
were frequently impressed. Not screenwriter Bob
Hopkins. He called Judy's tears "a Hollywood bath."

Anita Loos

Judy Garland: a vibrato in search of a voice.

Oscar Levant

I always thought Liza Minnelli's face deserving of
first prize in a beagle category.

John Simon

Paul Newman has eyes like chips of frozen sky.

Clive James

Charlotte Rampling's eyes are the precise color of a
turned-off television screen.

Sally Vincent

Audrey Hepburn gives the distinct impression she can
spell schizophrenia.

Billy Wilder

Goldie Hawn was landed with an idiot giggle, a remorseless inclination to squeak and if a brain hummed behind those dumbfounded eyes the secret never leaked out.

Donald Zec

Today's heroines are all like Jane Fonda.

Anita Loos

Roberto Benigni calls himself an Italian Donald Duck. I'd say he's an Italian furby.

Steven Spielberg

When they say, "Benigni, what a buffoon," it's as though they had called me a genius.

Roberto Benigni

I'm just a hair away from being a serial killer.

Dennis Hopper

Oh God! She looks like a chicken.

Truman Capote on Meryl Streep

I don't think I have the kind of face that makes an audience love you. And in the movies with all of those close-ups, that's very important. I think I look like Dame Edith Sitwell.

Meryl Streep

I can't say anything bad about Meryl Streep—and I love to say bad things about people.

James Woods

I'll never put Tom Cruise down. He's already kinda short.

Don Simpson

I wish I was taller. I probably look taller 'cos I've got such a big mouth.

Madonna

If I were an inch taller, I'd make another $150,000 a movie.

Gordon MacRae

Not since Attila the Hun swept across Europe leaving 500 years of blackness has there been a man like Lee Marvin.

Joshua Logan

Sylvester Stallone has a face that would look well upon a three-toed sloth.

Russell Davies

Cedric Hardwicke had the personality and drive of an old tortoise hunting for lettuce.

Rachel Roberts

Mel Tolkin looks like a stork that dropped a baby and broke it and is coming to explain to the parents.

Mel Brooks

George Hamilton is audibly tan.

Fran Lebowitz

133

You could put all the talent I had in your left eye and still not suffer from impaired vision.

Veronica Lake

I was the worst actor I ever came across.

Michael Wilding

I've done an awful lot of stuff that's a monument to public patience.

Tyrone Power

I've done my bit for motion pictures. I've stopped making them.

Liberace

Jean-Claude Van Damme exudes the charisma of a packet of Cup-A-Soup.

Jonathan Romney

I was beastly but never coarse. A high-class sort of heel.

George Sanders

George Sanders had a face, even in his 20s, which looked as though he had rented it on a long lease and had lived in it so long he didn't want to move out.

David Niven

Peter O'Toole has a face not so much lived in as infested.

Paul Taylor

Paul Henreid looks as though his idea of fun would be to find a nice cold damp grave and sit in it.

Richard Winnington

Jack Lemmon has a gift for butchering good parts while managing to look intelligent, thus constituting Hollywood's answer to the theater.

Wilfred Sheed

Jack Lemmon is not one of those actors who'll bore you to death discussing acting. He'd rather bore you to death discussing golf.

George Cukor

Mitch had a way of walking that was pure panther.

Polly Bergen on Robert Mitchum

People think I have an interesting walk. I'm just trying to hold my stomach in.

Robert Mitchum

I gave up being serious about making pictures about the time I made a film with Greer Garson and she took 127 takes to say no.

Robert Mitchum

Sean Connery? I'm looking for Commander James Bond, not an overgrown stunt man.

Ian Fleming

Playing James Bond? Sometimes I wear a white
dinner jacket, sometimes a black one.

Roger Moore

I've never had to say more than, "My name is Bond,
James Bond." That's the longest speech I ever had.

Roger Moore

Pierce Brosnan is an exceptionally handsome man,
but he always reminds me of the models in men's
knitwear catalogues.

Paul Hoggart

James Bond comes into my bathroom while I am
taking a shower and I say, "Pass me something to
slip on." And he passes my slippers.

Luciana Paluzzi, Bond girl in Thunderball

The James Bond film formula is: think of a theme
park with ten great rides and no waiting.

John Patterson

The stunts in The World is Not Enough are
disappointing. A "high-speed" power-boat chase
on the Thames looks slow and damp, leaving
Pierce Brosnan drenched, like a grumpy step-dad
persuaded against his will to get on a ride at
Alton Towers.

Peter Bradshaw

In The Avengers I had a few scenes with Sean
Connery but they weren't very big. It wasn't, "You
talkin' to me? You talkin' to me? I don't see anybody
else here." It was more like, "You're obviously not
talking to me as I have no lines."

Eddie Izzard

I'm not one of my favorite actors.

Charles Bronson

Charles Bronson's popularity within the movie
industry is not legendary.

David Shipman

There have always been mixed opinions about
Charles Bronson. Some people hate him like poison
and some people just hate him regular.

Jill Ireland

Someday I'd like a part where I can lean my elbow
against a mantelpiece and have a cocktail.

Charles Bronson

Working with Cher was like being in a blender with
an alligator.

Peter Bogdanovich

Lana Turner could give you an eyewitness account of
the Crucifixion and still put you to sleep.

Herman Mankiewicz

I have a face that would stop a sundial.

Charles Laughton

Charles Laughton's smile is that of a small boy
jovially peeping at life in a nudist colony.

Kenneth Tynan

Charles Laughton is always hovering somewhere,
waiting to be offended.

Peter Ustinov

We'd see Charles Laughton floating in his pool and it
was just the reverse of an iceberg—90% of him was
visible.

Peter Ustinov

Cagney had a quality of authenticity. Bogie was a big
fraud. Jimmy used to call him the Park Avenue tough
guy.

Pat O'Brien

When James Cagney hits a friend over the ear with a
revolver-butt, he does it as casually as he will
presently press the elevator button on his way out.

Kenneth Tynan

Cagney, Edward G. Robinson, Paul Muni—none of
them could hold a candle to Pacino when Pacino's
playing a gangster. He's like a male Bette Davis on
the rampage.

Lawrence J. Quirk

Woody Allen

The world's most famous dirty old man.

Joe Queenan

Woody Allen is a slight man with a startled look
about him, as if just caught in an unspeakable act.

Phil Berger, 1977

A face that convinces you God is a cartoonist.

Jack Kroll

I like Woody Allen because he's short. He's bald. He's
ugly. He can't get laid. He's just like me.

French taxi-driver

In reality, the "Woody" of Allen's films is as remote
from the real man as was "the Little Tramp" from the
millionaire autocrat, social climber and priapic
fancier of nymphets who was Chaplin.

John Baxter

The Woody Allen character that appears on the
screen is a Greek god version of what he's like in real
life. I met him once and he tried to hide behind Mia
Farrow.

John Cleese

He's not shy. He's anti-social. That's a different ball-
game.

Maureen Stapleton

How are you enjoying your power?

Woody Allen to the Queen on being introduced at the Royal Command Performance of Casino Royale

Woody wooing someone half his age is a lot less creepy when he is in ant form.

Christopher Tookey on Antz

To try to perk up his image, he has smiled and chatted with the media. Somehow, Woody being out-going and approachable seems way more grisly than his marrying someone who probably wanted a pony ride at their reception.

Libby Gelman-Waxner

The source of Allen's popularity has always escaped me; I find him a very thin slice of Harold Lloyd on rye.

Robert Hatch

When Woody Allen and his band were in London on their tour, I went to hear him play his clarinet. It was the first time he ever made me laugh.

Unnamed music expert

Fred Astaire

If I'm the Marlon Brando of dancing, he's the Cary Grant.

Gene Kelly

He even chews gum in time.

Stanley Donen

You know what his secret was? He knew what to leave out.

Hermes Pan, choreographer

When you've danced with Cyd Charisse you stay danced with.

Fred Astaire

When Ginger Rogers danced with Astaire, it was the only time in the movies when you looked at the man, not the woman.

Gene Kelly

He gives her class and she gives him sex.

Katharine Hepburn on Astaire and Rogers

I did everything Fred Astaire did—except backwards and in high heels.

Ginger Rogers

Watching the non-dancing, non-singing Fred Astaire is like watching a grounded skylark.

Vincent Canby

Fred Astaire will never say, though he's always asked, which of his dancing ladies was his favorite partner. If you ask me, he preferred the solo turns.

Vera-Ellen

Times change. In 1968, during the making of
Finian's Rainbow, Francis Coppola asked me, "Can
you find some way to make Fred Astaire dance a
little less like Fred Astaire?"

Hermes Pan

Tallulah Bankhead

I suppose you could say that Tallulah was a tramp, in
the elegant sense.

Tennessee Williams

Her voice has more timbre than Yellowstone National
Park.

John Crosby

I'm the foe of moderation, the champion of excess. If
I may lift a line from a die-hard whose identity is
lost in the shuffle, "I'd rather be strongly wrong than
weakly right."

Tallulah Bankhead

I've staged shows that called for the management
of a herd of buffalo, and I've shot actors out of
cannons for 50 feet into the arms of an adagio
dancer, but both of them were easier than saying
"Good morning" to Miss Bankhead.

Billy Rose

I'm not childless, dahling. I'm child-free.

Tallulah Bankhead

142

I have only two temperamental outbursts a year—
each lasts six months.

Tallulah Bankhead

--You're impossible!
--Who wants to be possible?

Friend and Tallulah Bankhead

I might offend morals, but never good taste—the
more important of the two.

Tallulah Bankhead

Tallulah was sitting in a group of people, giving the
monologue she always thought was conversation.

Lillian Hellman

Tallulah talked so ceaselessly that you had to make a
reservation five minutes ahead to get a word in.

Earl Wilson

Tallulah never bored anyone, and I consider that
humanitarianism of a very high order indeed.

Anita Loos

Tallulah is always skating on thin ice, and everyone
wants to be there when it breaks.

Mrs Patrick Campbell

I read Shakespeare and the Bible, and I can shoot
dice. That's what I call a liberal education.

Tallulah Bankhead

I was acting opposite Marlon Brando in Rampant Eagle. I asked if we could change the title because the only thing rampant about the goddamn thing was Brando's crabs.

Tallulah Bankhead

Nobody can be exactly like me. Sometimes even I have trouble doing it.

Tallulah Bankhead

It's the good girls who keep diaries. The bad girls never have the time.

Tallulah Bankhead

If I had my life to live over again, I'd make all the same mistakes—only sooner.

Tallulah Bankhead

Codeine! Bourbon!

Tallulah Bankhead, her last words

Tallulah who?

Beatrice Lillie

Humphrey Bogart

Humphrey Bogart is probably the most subtle bad man (genus American) the films have produced.

Otis Ferguson

Bogart can be tough without a gun...all he has to do to dominate a scene is to enter it.

Raymond Chandler

Wry, detached, anti-Establishment, a man with the sure masculinity of a whiskey straight. Bogart was unflinching, outspoken, cynical and a realist; a tough guy in a trenchcoat, a man's man.

David Zinman

Bogart's a helluva nice guy till 11.30pm. After that he thinks he's Bogart.

Dave Chasen

Me hit a woman? Why, I'm too sweet and chivalrous. Besides, it's dangerous.

Humphrey Bogart

When I started out, I was always the guy behind the guy behind the gun.

Humphrey Bogart

When a woman appealed to him, Bogart waited for her like the flame waits for the moth.

Louise Brooks

I did nothing in Casablanca that I hadn't done in twenty movies before that and suddenly they discover I'm sexy. Any time that Ingrid Bergman looks at a man, he has sex appeal.

Humphrey Bogart

Richard Burton
The Frank Sinatra of Shakespeare.

Elizabeth Taylor

There is nothing the British like better than a bloke who comes from nowhere, makes it, and then gets clobbered.

Melvyn Bragg

A spoiled genius from the Welsh gutter, a drunk, a womanizer. It's rather an attractive image.

Richard Burton

I always get an attack of piles on the third week of shooting and my back slips.

Richard Burton

Charlie Chaplin

I am known in parts of the world by people who have never heard of Jesus Christ.

Charlie Chaplin

Chaplin is no businessman—all he knows is that he can't take anything less.

Sam Goldwyn

A second-rate bicycle-acrobat who should have kept his mouth shut.

Kingsley Amis

When he found a voice to say what was on his mind, he was like a child of eight writing lyrics for Beethoven's Ninth.

Billy Wilder

146

Chaplin means more to me than the idea of God.

François Truffaut

When I see a bowler hat it is not Chaplin I think
of, but the more lovable and humanly engaging
personalities of Laurel and Hardy.

Barry Humphries

Gary Cooper

I came to Hollywood for one reason and one reason
alone: to fuck that divine Gary Cooper.

Tallulah Bankhead

For all his quiet speech and diffident ways, Coop
might have been the Babe Ruth of the boudoir
league. It was whispered down the studio corridors
that he had the endowments of Hercules and the
staying power of Job.

Budd Schulberg

All I can say is he's hung like a horse and can go all
night.

Clara Bow

Coop was reading *Along Came Jones*, the story I was
adapting for him to star in. I bumped into him in
the studio commissary and asked him how he liked
the book. "Oh, fine," he said, "I'm half way through
it. I'm reading it word by word."

Nunnally Johnson

Gary Cooper got a reputation as a great actor just by thinking hard about the next line.

King Vidor

If you ask me if I am the luckiest guy in the world, all I can say is "Yup."

Gary Cooper

Joan Crawford

As a human being Joan Crawford is a very great actress.

Nicholas Ray

Joan Crawford would have made an exemplary prison matron, possibly at Buchenwald.

Harriet Van Horne

Joan even had a special outfit just for answering her fan mail.

Shelley Winters

A cheap flapper who liked to get laid.

Louis B. Mayer

Joan Crawford would knit continually while rehearsing, eating, arguing, and looking at rushes. "Do you knit when you fuck?" Oscar Levant asked her. There were icebergs on the set of Humoresque for ages after that.

Jean Negulesco

She should have had puppies, not children.

Oscar Levant

Joan asked me to squire her to a play in LA. I said,
"But you've already seen this play." "Yes," she said,
"but not in this dress."

Clark Gable

Miss Crawford's bigger-than-life lips have the color
and splash and latitude of a split persimmon. More
so even than the eyes, this labial flamboyancy is her
most arresting feature.

Cecil Beaton

I think she is a splendid actress, but I am a little
repulsed by her shining lips, like balloon tires in wet
weather.

John Betjeman

I'd rather have a cannibal for a co-star.

Anthony Perkins

Toward the end of her life she looked like a hungry
insect magnified a million times—a praying mantis
that had forgotten how to pray.

Quentin Crisp

Bette Davis

Take away the pop eyes, the cigarette, and those
funny clipped words and what have you got?

Joan Crawford

149

All she had going for her was her talent.

David Zinman

She knew how to fill a room with her magnificent arrogance.

Richard Corliss

I walked onto the set of All About Eve on the first day and said, "Good morning," and do you know her reply? She said, "Oh shit, good manners." I never spoke to her again—ever.

Celeste Holm

—If you hadn't have been an actress, what would you have wanted to be?
—A man.

Hedda Hopper and Bette Davis

I was the first actress who ever came out of the water looking wet.

Bette Davis

—I hate Joan Crawford. She couldn't act, she was a whore!
—Miss Davis, excuse me. Miss Crawford was a great star and a great lady, besides which she is dead. You should never speak ill of the dead.
—Just because someone's dead doesn't mean they've changed.

Bette Davis and Interviewer

It seemed to me that each one coveted what the other possessed. Joan envied Bette's incredible talent, and Bette envied Joan's seductive glamour.

George Cukor

Bette was the better actress but Joan had better clothes.

Madonna

Well, dear, I think we've had the best of her.
Mae West to her escort after her second meeting with Bette Davis

Bette Davis got most of her exercise by putting her foot down.

Tom Shales

Surely nobody but a mother could have loved Bette Davis at the height of her career.

Brian Aherne

If I ever get hold of that hag I'll tear every hair out of her moustache.

Tallulah Bankhead

Marlene Dietrich

Your name begins with a caress and ends with the crack of a whip.

Jean Cocteau

She was Mother Teresa, only with better legs.

Billy Wilder

151

The most striking of her features is her whiteness,
which would put the moon or a white rabbit to
shame. Instead of eyebrows, she has limned
butterflies' antennae on her forehead.

Cecil Beaton

The relationship between the make-up man and the
film actor is that of accomplices in crime.

Marlene Dietrich

Everything about her seems quaint and Germanic—
including her Wagnerian self-love. There is always
a fascination about people who manage to exist
beyond the period in which they were appropriate
symbols—a little like the Walt Disney animals who
run off a cliff and walk on air for a few moments
before they discover it.

Maximilian Schell

Douglas Fairbanks Sr

Douglas Fairbanks was a complete fantasy, not like
Disney's which has an overlayer of whimsy and
sophistication, but unashamed and joyous.
Balustrades were made to be vaulted, draperies
to be a giant slide, chandeliers to swing from,
citadels to be scaled.

Frank S. Nugent

Doug's physical energy was the perfect center for
fast-moving, breezy films that took the business of
making films rather lightly and showed how easily
human error can be corrected with a little zest, a
little effort, and a lot of jumping around.

Gerald Mast

Fairbanks died aged 56, his tanned body apparently
untouched by age but actually so muscle-bound that
the blood could barely circulate. He had not so much
died, some friends thought, as run down.

John Baxter

W.C. Fields

Though he looked like a brimming Toby Jug, it was
always clear that no mantelpiece would hold him.

Kenneth Tynan

A Merry Christmas to all my friends except two.

W. C. Fields in a display ad in *Variety*

His voice, nasal, tinny, and massively bored, is that
of a prisoner who has been uselessly affirming his
innocence in the same court for centuries.

Kenneth Tynan

He moved mountains until they fell on him, and then
brushed himself off and looked around for more.

Otis Ferguson

His main purpose seemed to be to break as many rules as possible and cause the maximum amount of trouble for everybody.

Robert Lewis Smith

Bill never really wanted to hurt anybody. He just felt an obligation.

Gregory La Cava

–Would you like to play golf with me?
–No, thanks, if I ever want to play with a prick, I'll play with my own.

Producer and W.C. Fields

Give him an evasive answer. Tell him to go fuck himself.

W.C. Fields

He has a profound respect for old age. Especially when it's bottled.

Gene Fowler on Fields's fondness for aged bourbon

Fields had his own ideas about playing Mr Micawber in David Copperfield. He wanted to include a juggling routine and when I said Dickens never mentioned Micawber juggling, he said, "He probably forgot."

George Cukor

Errol Flynn

A magnificent specimen of the rampant male.

David Niven

No actor swashed so blithe a buckle.

David Shipman

If I have any genius, it is a genius for living.

Errol Flynn

His life was a fifty-year trespass against good taste.

Leslie Mallory

I allow myself to be understood as a colorful
fragment in a drab world.

Errol Flynn

You always knew where you were with Errol. He
always let you down.

David Niven

I'm glad you're going to be photographing me on
the new movie, Jack. Don't worry about this fat
round my middle. I'll fuck it off in three days.

Errol Flynn to Jack Cardiff, cinematographer

When I was 11, I got the part of this little Indian kid
in Kim and Errol Flynn was playing the other guy.
The first day of shooting, I went on the set with my
mother and an elderly lady studio teacher. Flynn
came up to us and somebody said, "This is Dean
Stockwell." He stuck out his hand and said, "Hi, kid.
Have you had your first fuck yet?" I just looked at
this guy, thinking, I finally found a friend.

Dean Stockwell

Errol Flynn is priapic! The man never stops! They should tell the birds and the bees about him.

Anita Louise

You know Flynn, he's either got to be fighting or fucking.

Jack L. Warner

Clark Gable

– How does it feel to be the world's greatest lover?
– It's a living.

Louella Parsons and Clark Gable

Clark Gable made you feel twice the woman you thought you were.

Ursula Theiss, wife of Robert Taylor

"King of Hollywood?" If Clark had an inch less he'd be called "Queen of Hollywood."

Carole Lombard, his wife

Women liked Gable best when he played a heavy with a grin.

Howard Hawks

Why do I prefer prostitutes? With one of these floozies, I don't have to pretend that I'm Clark Gable.

Clark Gable

The only reason the fans come to see me is that I know life is great and they know I know it.

Clark Gable

Clark is the sort of guy, if you say, "Hiya Clark, how are yah?" he's stuck for an answer.

Ava Gardner

Clark Gable has enemies all right—but they all like him.

David O. Selznick

He had a magnificent array of dazzling teeth. These were made by a dentist named Wallace and were known as the Wallace Collection.

Lilli Palmer

Greta Garbo

Garbo. No. Garbo! Better.

Garson Kanin

What, when drunk, one sees in other women, one sees in Garbo sober.

Kenneth Tynan

At a party in Hollywood, I was introduced to Greta Garbo and was somewhat dismayed to see that she was in color.

S.J. Perelman

Every man's harmless fantasy mistress. She gave you the impression that, if your imagination had to sin, it could at least congratulate itself on its impeccable taste.

Alistair Cooke

If snowbound for a night in a wooden shed with
Miss Garbo, all the men I have ever known would
have been terrified.

Quentin Crisp

She made you eat a mile of her shit, just to get a
whiff of her asshole.

John Gilbert

–How would you like to come out for dinner with me
on Monday?
–How do I know I'm going to be hungry on Monday?

Howard Dietz and Greta Garbo

Like Gone With the Wind, Garbo is monumentally
overrated. Her voice is deep, she has no humor,
her figure is flat, her carriage is not graceful,
her feet are big, her private life is a fog. Only
her face is perfect.

Alfred Hitchcock

Greta Garbo is hermaphroditic, with the cold quality
of a mermaid.

Tennessee Williams

She has the air of an aspirin addict; she still wears
the perpetual headache which once seemed so
intriguing in the deaf and dumb pictures.

Matthew Josephson on Grand Hotel

The cinema has given precisely one great artist to the world: Greta Garbo—unless you count that damn mouse.

Louis B. Mayer

Cary Grant

Cary Grant made men seem like a good idea.

Graham McCann

Hollywood's lone example of the Sexy Gentleman.

Tom Wolfe

Everybody wants to be Cary Grant. Even I want to be Cary Grant.

Cary Grant

—Who does the best Cary Grant impression?
—I do.

Interviewer and Cary Grant

His suntan looks like it was done on a rotisserie.

Melvin Maddocks

Everyone tells me I've had such an interesting life, but sometimes I think it's been nothing but stomach disturbances and self-concern.

Cary Grant

He was lucky, and he knew it.

Cary Grant, proposed epitaph

Rex Harrison

If Rex Harrison weren't the second-best high
comedian in the country, all he'd be fit for would be
selling second-hand cars in Great Portland Street.

Noël Coward

Rex rang my secretary last month, and asked her
sharply, "Where's your boss?" When she replied, "On
safari," he snapped, "Well, I hope he meets a hungry
lion."

Alan J. Lerner

Nobody is as interesting to spend an evening with as
a really good part.

Rex Harrison

During The Agony and the Ecstasy, I played a scene
with Rex in which we were walking together
through a cathedral. "Have you noticed," said Rex,
"we're being lit by only one spotlight?" "Yes," I
replied, "I have noticed." "Well, get out of it," he
snarled.

Richard Pearson

On Rex's 70th birthday, I suggested we hire a
telephone box and invite all his friends to a party.

Doug Hayward

The only enduring relationship Rex Harrison had
was with his basset hound, Homer.

Elizabeth Rees-Harrison, ex-wife

What has Rex Harrison ever done for England,
except live abroad, refuse to pay his taxes, and
call everybody a cunt?

Harold French on the announcement of Rex's knighthood

Katharine Hepburn

—I think I am too tall for you.

—Don't worry, Miss Hepburn, I'll soon cut you down
to my size.

Katharine Hepburn and Spencer Tracy

I always admired Katharine Hepburn's cheekbones.
More than her films.

Bette Davis

She has a face that belongs to the sea and the wind,
with large rocking horse nostrils and teeth that you
just know bite an apple every day.

Cecil Beaton

I can't imagine Rhett Butler chasing you for ten years.

**David O. Selznick turning her down for the role of
Scarlett O'Hara**

Katharine Hepburn isn't really stand-offish. She
ignores everyone equally.

Lucille Ball

I doubt in her entire life she's ever bought lunch for herself or anyone else. Which is the sole detail I care to offer.

Ralph Richardson

Bob Hope

You spell Bob Hope, C-L-A-S-S.

Lucille Ball

There's nothing I wouldn't do for Bing, and there's nothing he wouldn't do for me. And that's the way we go through life—doing nothing for each other.

Bob Hope

Hope is not a comedian. He just translates what others write for him.

Groucho Marx

Bob Hope is a funny guy, but if he was drowning he couldn't ad lib, "Help!"

Hal Kanter

Over the past 50 years Bob Hope employed 88 joke-writers...who supplied him with more than one million gags. And he still couldn't make me laugh.

Eddie Murphy

Marx Bros.

Now there sits a man with an open mind. You can feel the draft from here.

Groucho Marx on Chico

Harpo was a man of very few words, except when it came to Scotch, horses and ladies. Actually, Scotch ran a poor third. Which wasn't easy considering the way his horses ran.

Groucho Marx

There were three things that Chico was always on—a phone, a horse or a broad.

Groucho Marx

If there was no action around, Chico would play solitaire and bet against himself.

Groucho Marx

Put in my coffin a deck of cards, a mashie niblick, and a pretty blonde.

Chico Marx, his last wishes

—How'd you like to write a script for the Marx brothers?

—I'd as soon write a script for the Barbary apes.

Sam Harris and George S. Kaufman

I never knew what bicarbonate of soda was until I wrote a Marx Brothers picture.

Herman Mankiewicz

Writing for the Marx brothers is an ordeal by fire. Make sure you wear asbestos pants.

Herman Mankiewicz to S.J. Perelman

The Marx Brothers and their various relatives
run around the stage for almost an hour. Why,
I'll never understand.

Lou Kramer, review of the Marx Brothers' vaudeville act

My sex life is now reduced to fan letters from an
elderly lesbian who would like to borrow $800.

Groucho Marx, aged 60

Tell me, doctor, did you ever fall out of a patient?

Groucho Marx to a tree surgeon

Groucho Marx has shaken hands with presidents,
danced cheek to cheek with Marlene Dietrich, played
baseball with Lou Gehrig, traded backhands with
Jack Kramer, strummed guitar duets with the great
Segovia, and he's insulted nearly everyone worth
insulting.

Arthur Marx on his father

This is what I want on my tombstone: Here lies
Groucho Marx, and lies and lies and lies. P.S. He
never kissed an ugly girl.

Groucho Marx

Marilyn Monroe

An arrogant little tail-twitcher who learned to throw
sex in your face.

Nunnally Johnson

She knew exactly her impact on men. And that's all.

Fritz Lang

Breasts she had. And a wiggly figure. But to me sex is class, something more than a wiggly behind. If it weren't, I know two hundred whores who would be stars.

Frank Capra

Marilyn Monroe conjures up two straws in a single soda, juke boxes, running nylons and drive-in movies for necking (does she not project a hypnotized nymphomania?).

Cecil Beaton

I am the only director who ever made two pictures with Marilyn Monroe. Forget the Oscar, I deserve the Purple Heart.

Billy Wilder

I have never met anyone as utterly mean as Marilyn Monroe. Nor as utterly fabulous on the screen, and that includes Garbo.

Billy Wilder

Marilyn used to carry around books of Marcel Proust, with their titles facing out, although I never saw her read any of them. She had not yet discovered Dostoevski's *Brothers Karamazov* and, in fact, had only lately discovered Hollywood's Brothers Warner.

Jack Paar

There's been an awful lot of crap written about
Marilyn Monroe, and I don't know, there may be
an exact psychiatric term for what was wrong with
her but truth to tell, I think she was quite mad.

George Cukor

–Tony Curtis said that kissing you was like kissing
Hitler.
–At least I look better in a dress than he does.

Interviewer and Marilyn Monroe

–Why can't you get here on time, for fuck's sake?
–Oh, do you have that word in England, too?

**Laurence Olivier and Marilyn Monroe on the set of The
Prince and the Showgirl**

After 50 takes, I'd take her to one side and say
kindly, "Don't worry, Marilyn," and she would
innocently reply, "Worry about what?"

Billy Wilder on The Seven Year Itch

It used to be you'd call her at 9am, she'd show up at
noon. Now you call her in May–she shows up in
October.

Billy Wilder

I'm not a dumb blonde this time. I'm a crazy dumb
blonde. And to think, Arthur did this to me.

**Marilyn Monroe on The Misfits written by her
third husband, Arthur Miller**

Marilyn Monroe auditioned a great deal, late
afternoons, in executive offices.

Joseph L. Mankiewicz

I have the most wonderful memory for forgetting
things.

Marilyn Monroe

Hollywood didn't kill Marilyn Monroe. It's the
Marilyn Monroes who are killing Hollywood.

Billy Wilder

–Why aren't you attending her funeral?
–Why should I? She won't be there.

Reporter and Arthur Miller

Jack Nicholson

A legend in his own lifetime and in his own mind.

Jennifer Lopez

He makes mischief and evil the most charming
things in the world.

Susan Anspach

I jump from immaculately polite to violent–there's
not much rudeness in between. Rudeness is for
amateurs.

Jack Nicholson

My best feature's my smile. And smiles–praise
heaven–don't get fat.

Jack Nicholson

–Why do you always wear the sunglasses?
–Without them, I'm fat and fifty. With them,
I'm Jack Nicholson.

Frank Ellroy and Jack Nicholson

Nicholson has to wear sunglasses 'cos he gets in his
own reflection, his aura is so great.

Billy Crystal

Jack Nicholson uses his sunglasses as Madame de
Pompadour once deployed a fan, a prop around
which he can peek and flirt and generally surprise
the hell out of everyone.

Allison Pearson

Arnold Schwarzenegger

If Arnie hadn't existed, we would have had to build
him.

John Millius

He's not an actor, he's a special effect.

Jonathan Coe

He's the only man in the world that it is impossible
to imagine having been a baby.

Penny Patrick

His acting is limited. He has an inability to pick
up light objects, such as a telephone, in any sort of
naturalistic way.

Nigel Andrews

168

I just use my muscles as a conversation piece, like someone walking a cheetah down 42nd Street.

Arnold Schwarzenegger

He's so lifelike!

George Carlin meeting Arnie for the first time

Arnold's acted in plenty of movies but spoken less dialogue that any actor except—maybe—Lassie.

Robin Williams

After Arnold Schwarzenegger, Dolph Lundgren is a bit of a disappointment. At least Arnold looks as if he comes supplied with batteries.

Adam Mars-Jones

Frank Sinatra

Frank and I were always great in bed. The trouble usually started on the way to the bidet.

Ava Gardner

Sinatra's idea of paradise is a place where there are plenty of women and no newspapermen. He doesn't know it, but he'd be better off if it was the other way around.

Humphrey Bogart

My advice to widows—don't sell the house and don't sleep with Frank Sinatra.

Lauren Bacall

I always knew Frank would end up in bed with a boy.

Ava Gardner on Mia Farrow

The Lovable Landmine.

Peter Lawford

Frank Sinatra is the kind of singer who comes along once in a lifetime—but why did it have to be my lifetime?

Bing Crosby

James Stewart

James Stewart is everything the British audience wants an American to be but so rarely is.

Anthony Quayle

Jimmy Stewart's appeal lay in being so unusually usual.

Frank Capra

If I had my career over again? Maybe I'd say to myself, speed it up a little.

James Stewart

When I watched Jimmy Stewart act, I felt like a triangle player in the orchestra who keeps watching the conductor and then, when he finally gets the baton signal, he misses the triangle.

Cary Grant

Barbra Streisand

To know her is not necessarily to love her.

Rex Reed

Working with Barbra Streisand is like sitting down to a picnic in the middle of a freeway.

Kris Kristofferson

Were she to collide with a Mac truck, it is the truck that would drop dead.

John Simon

For our interview she personally hired the director, supervised the lighting, fixed the camera angles and organized the flowers. She would have had time to grow them because she kept us waiting five hours without a sign of apology.

Clive James

Barbra Streisand takes every ballad and turns it into a three-act opera.

Truman Capote

Elizabeth Taylor

If I'd had a face like Elizabeth Taylor's I would never have won two Oscars.

Bette Davis

All my life I wanted to look like Liz Taylor. Now I find that Liz Taylor is beginning to look like me.

Divine

Liz Taylor says she's retaining water. And so is the Hoover Dam.

Lou Berne

I've never really thought of myself as an actress.

Elizabeth Taylor

Some of my best leading men have been horses and dogs.

Elizabeth Taylor

I remember my brother once saying, "I'd like to marry Elizabeth Taylor," and my father said, "Don't worry, your turn will come."

Spike Milligan

Orson Welles

It's like meeting God without dying.

Dorothy Parker

I am an actor on the stage, screen and radio. I write, and I'm a director. Also I'm a producer. I'm only sorry there are so many of me, and so few of you.

Orson Welles giving a lecture to a small audience

When I have seen him and talked with him, I feel like a plant that has been watered.

Marlene Dietrich

There, but for the grace of God, goes God.

Herman Mankiewicz

Steven Spielberg paid $60,000 for the "Rosebud" sledge. Not that he would pay me that to write a script.

Orson Welles

Mae West

A milestone, a catchword, sex with its tongue in its cheek.

Marlene Dietrich

A plumber's idea of Cleopatra.

W.C. Fields

The ultimate female impersonator.

Divine

–How do you do, Miss West.
–How do you do what?

Red Skelton and Mae West

She stole everything but the cameras.

George Raft on her film debut in Night After Night

I never meant "Come up and see me sometime," to be sexy.

Mae West

It isn't what I do, but how I do it. It isn't what I say, but how I say it. And how I look when I do it and say it.

Mae West

Mae West told me she was working on a new play. I enquired what it was about and she replied, "It's about this guy. He's a cock-sucker and—" Shocked, I made a hasty excuse and left. When I told the story to Noël Coward he said, "I have never heard a plot begin so promisingly."

Charles Cochran

Proof of her greatness lies in the fact that the line, "Come up and see me sometime," has passed for ever into the folklore of filth because of her delivery of the phrase—which, in itself, contains not one word that a nun would be reluctant to utter.

Quentin Crisp

Even at 70, Miss West still possesses overwhelming sexual force. It comes and goes like distant music heard across a fairground on a summer night— but it is still there.

Saturday Evening Post

I'm the one who changed my name from May to Mae. I didn't like that "y" hanging down below the line. I don't like anything downbeat.

Mae West

Mae West couldn't sing a lullaby without making it sound sexy.

Noah Beery

174

FAME

CELEBRITY

A celebrity is a person who works hard all his life to become well known and then goes through back streets wearing dark glasses to avoid being recognized.

Fred Allen

A sign of celebrity is that his name is often worth more than his services.

Daniel J. Boorstin

Being a celebrity never helped me to make a good film or command the audience of my daughter. It doesn't even seem to keep fleas off our dogs—and if it won't give one the advantage over a couple of fleas, then I guess there can't be much in being a celebrity after all.

Walt Disney

A pleasant feeling is always generated by the demise of a celebrity. It proves to the envious that, ultimately, the stars are only our equals, or we theirs if we can just find a significant way to die.

Quentin Crisp

FAME

Dahling, I have enemies I've never even met. That's fame!

Tallulah Bankhead

If you don't already know who someone is, why on earth would you want to meet him?

Eva Gabor

Since becoming famous, I get to torture a better class of man.

Sharon Stone

When I started out I didn't have any desire to be an actress or to learn how to act. I just wanted to be famous.

Katharine Hepburn

Writing a good movie brings a writer about as much fame as steering a bicycle.

Ben Hecht

Don't confuse fame with success. One is Madonna; the other is Helen Keller.

Erma Bombeck

The final test of fame is to have a crazy person imagine he is you.

Mel Brooks

STARDOM

Stardom? I never touch the stuff.

John Lithgow

Half the people in Hollywood are dying to be
discovered and the other half are afraid they will be.

Ethel Barrymore

–How did you become a movie star?
–I wanted to.

Robert Morley and Norma Shearer

In Hollywood, unknown actors wear sunglasses in
the hope of being mistaken for knowns.

Richard E. Grant

All of a sudden, you become Jesus.

James Caan

Some movie stars wear their sunglasses even in
church; they're afraid God might recognize them and
ask for autographs.

Fred Allen

The reason stars are good, they walk through a door
and they think, "Everybody wants to lay me."

Howard Hawks

People want to fuck movie stars and hug television
stars.

Ted Danson

You're not a star until they can spell your name in
Karachi.

Humphrey Bogart

Until you're known in my profession as a monster
you're not a star.

Bette Davis

When they say you're a faggot, that's when you
know you're a star.

Jack Nicholson

Stars are small people with big heads.

Gore Vidal

A star is someone you don't mind spending two
hours in the cinema with—even if the film is bad.

Claude Lelouch

My idea of a movie star is Joan Crawford, who can
chew up two directors and three producers before
lunch.

Shelley Winters

Stars are people who sit in their trailers demanding
all-green jelly beans.

Greg Kinnear

Stars are people who sell a lot of popcorn.

Harrison Ford

A lotta cats copy the *Mona Lisa*, but people still line
up to see the original.

Louis Armstrong

When people see me on the street all the guys think
I look like somebody who was in the army with
them, and all the women think I look like their
first husband.

Bob Newhart

I hate the word "superstar." I have never been able to
think in those terms. They are overstatements. You
don't hear them speak of Shakespeare as a superpoet.
You don't hear them call Michelangelo a super-
painter. They only apply the word to this mundane
market.

James Cagney

Ah, stardom... They put your name on a star in the
sidewalk on Hollywood Boulevard and you walk
down and find a pile of dog-shit on it. That tells the
whole story, baby.

Lee Marvin

Stardom is all hard work, aspirins and purgatives.

Elsa Lanchester

You need to be a bit of a bastard to be a star.

Laurence Olivier

If you're not everything to everybody, you're nobody
in Hollywood.

Robert Evans

It was W.S. Gilbert who said "When everybody's somebody then no one's anybody."

David Niven

We can't all be heroes. Someone has to sit on the kerb and clap as they go by.

Will Rogers

Stars live in a cocoon of praise. They never meet the people who don't like them.

Robert Morley

Fans are people who let an actor know he's not alone in the way he feels about himself.

Jack Carson

The girls went crazy for Frank Sinatra. They hid in his dressing room. In the trunk of his car. When it snowed, they fought over his footprints, which some took home and stored in refrigerators.

Arnold Shaw

Any star can be devoured by human adoration, sparkle by sparkle.

Shirley Temple

I've had lots of fan mail but I do remember one abusive letter. It wasn't signed but it had a P.S.— "If undelivered, please forward to Demi Moore."

Geena Davis

I can walk down the street as anyone and not be recognized, but if I walk down the street as Marilyn Monroe, I am.

Marilyn Monroe

For many years I could walk the streets unrecognized except by people who thought I was Dustin Hoffman.

Al Pacino

I've signed Meg Ryan's autograph more often than my own. If anyone comes up and says Sleepless in Seattle was their favorite, I just sign Meg Ryan.

Melanie Griffith

People come up to me and say, "What's it like being married to Antonio Banderas?" And I say, "Terrific. He's great in bed."

Meg Ryan

–Name?
–Cary Grant.
–You don't look like Cary Grant.
–Nobody does.

Studio security guard and Cary Grant

–You're Steve Martin, aren't you? Know you anywhere. Seen all your movies. What can I do for you?
–I'd like to withdraw $200.
–Certainly. I'll need to see some identification.

Steve Martin and bank clerk

A fan came over during dinner one time and Bogey told him to beat it. When the guy got back to his table I heard his companion say, quite happily, "See, I told ya he'd insult ya."

Nunnally Johnson

Go away, dear, I don't need you anymore.

Norma Talmadge, retired actress, to an autograph hunter

Woody Allen and I are having lunch in a New York cafeteria. A middle-aged woman comes up and says to him, "Are you Woody Allen?" Woody mumbles, "Yes." She goes back to her table then a moment later comes back and says, "Are you sure you're Woody Allen?"

Ralph Rosenblum

—Are you Peter Sellers?
—Not today.

Fan and Peter Sellers

—Are you the Tallulah Bankhead?
—What's left of her.

Airport customs official and Tallulah Bankhead

—Are you Robert Mitchum?
—Well, somebody has to be.

Fan and Robert Mitchum

All warts, thick lenses, terminal dandruff—typical Mitchum fans.

Robert Mitchum

—It's Walter Matthau! I thought you were dead.
—Not if you look closely.

Fan and Walter Matthau

I never met a single person who lived the way the public believed we lived.

Blanche Yurka

Being a star has made it possible for me to get insulted in places where the average Negro could never hope to get insulted.

Sammy Davis Jr

People would stop John Belushi in the street for his autograph and he'd say, "What's your name?" They'd say, "Jason." He'd write, "Jason, grow up. John Belushi."

Donald Sutherland

—As the wife of Rex Harrison you enjoyed a star's lifestyle. Do you miss that life...the glamor, the fancy hotels, the lavish parties, the chauffeur-driven car?
—No, but I miss the chauffeur.

Reporter and Rachel Roberts

Movies are full of people who project a mysterious something on the screen that is entirely absent when you meet them.

Dick Cavett

Producers and directors like to be associated with
stars. They love to sit at dinner parties with them.
It's the starfucker phenomenon.

David Puttnam

If you can make a star out of Steven Seagal, you can
make a star out of anyone.

Mike Bygrave

Stardom gave me everything I never wanted.

Ava Gardner

Stars are a pain in the ass to a director. Their egos
need to be stroked 24 hours a day. Ultimately what
they do is waste time and time is the enemy of all
production.

William Goldman

If there were a way to make movies without actors,
George Lucas would do it.

Mark Hamill

I never go out unless I look like Joan Crawford the
movie star. If you want to see the girl next door, go
next door.

Joan Crawford

Even in her bath, Joan Crawford looked as if she
were about to make a public appearance, just in case
a crowd happened to drop by.

Raddie Harris

One of the main things about being successful is that I stopped being afraid of dying. When you're a movie star you're already dead, you're embalmed.

Dustin Hoffman

If I hadn't been a star I would have been a beautician or a missionary.

Dolly Parton

Never take top billing. You'll last longer that way.

Bill Cosby

In all our films together I always took second billing. Garson Kanin once asked Spencer, "Didn't you ever hear of ladies first?" and Spence replied, "This is a movie, not a lifeboat."

Katharine Hepburn

At last I get top billing.

Wallace Ford, character actor, proposed epitaph

Two of the cruellest, most primitive punishments our town deals out to those who have fallen from favor are the empty mailbox and the silent telephone.

Hedda Hopper

In Hollywood you can be forgotten while you're out of the room going to the toilet.

Dustin Hoffman

Sooner or later a public figure becomes a public bore or a public joke.

Richard Burton

This year I'm a star, but what will I be next year—
a black hole?

Woody Allen

There is nothing worse than being famous and broke.
Kim Basinger

What stars fear most is the death of their fame, and
most would rather be infamous than go back to
anonymity. The worst thing you could possible say to
a star would be, "Didn't you used to be famous?"
Truman Capote

—Such a week...first my darling Edith Piaf's
funeral...the crowds mob me, in spite of my three
black veils...then my darling Jean Cocteau's
funeral...six veils, but again they mob me...
When I get home I ask myself what will it be
like at my funeral?
—Why don't you try dying at sea, Marlene?
Marlene Dietrich and Emlyn Williams

In the final analysis, it's true that fame is
unimportant. No matter how great a man is, the
size of his funeral usually depends on the weather.
Rosemary Clooney

PUBLICITY & ADVERTISING

Publicity can be terrible. But only if you don't have any.
Jane Russell

People living in Hollywood have to stay home if they're in a foul mood; anything outside the home is potential publicity.

Jeremy Brett

'Tis better to have loved and divorced than never to have had any publicity at all.

Ava Gardner

Hugh Grant and Liz Hurley have been going through a bad patch, but they've decided to stay together for the sake of the media.

Frank Skinner after the Divine Brown indiscretion

All publicity is good, except an obituary notice.

Brendan Behan

To the unwashed public, Joan Collins is a star. But to those who know her, she's a commodity who would sell her own bowel movement.

Anthony Newley, ex-husband

After a while the stars believe their own publicity. I've never met a grateful performer in the film business.

Harry Cohn

It's not what you are in Hollywood—it's what people think you are.

Robert Stack

You can fool all the people all the time if the
advertising is right and the budget is big enough.

Joseph E. Levine

Given the right P.R., armpit hair on actresses could
become a national fetish.

Lenny Bruce

Wanna know what the summer's blockbuster
is going to be? See who McDonald's does the
marketing tie-in with. Wanna know what blockbuster will do disappointing business? See who
Burger King ties in with.

Dawson E. Rambo

They actually brought out a bubble bath container
that looked like me. You twisted my head off and
poured liquid from my neck—lovely or what?

Carrie Fisher, Princess Leia in Star Wars

For Batman Forever, Kenner Products got Warner
Bros to put the Riddler in tights because baggy pants
don't look good on toy action figures.

Rick Watkins, toy development manager

A Bond movie is not made. It is packaged. Like an
Almond Joy. So much coconut to this much chocolate
and a dash of raisins.

Joseph Gelmis

The World is Not Enough is a state-of-the-art commercial for more products than are advertised in all the TV breaks during the Super Bowl. One of Bond's gadgets is even disguised as a Visa credit card.

Boyd Farrow

You get the feeling that if the Wizard of Oz were remade today the yellow brick road would be brought to you courtesy of Carpeteria.

Peter Rainier

GOSSIP & THE MEDIA

Gossip is the new pornography.

Woody Allen

Gossip is hearing something you like about someone you don't.

Earl Wilson

Probably the biggest topics of gossip in Hollywood are who's gay, who's getting divorced and who's had plastic surgery.

Gilda Radner

It's impossible to keep a secret in Hollywood. The star tells the producer, the producer tells the hooker and then it goes straight to the press.

Luke Morton

Never believe anything until it is officially denied.

Claud Cockburn

Ninety per cent of the moving pictures exhibited in America are so vulgar, witless and dull that it is preposterous to write about them in any publication not intended to be read while chewing gum.

Wolcott Gibbs

The success of *People* magazine was explained by Jeff Goldblum in The Big Chill: nothing in it takes longer to read than the average crap.

Sean Penn

Younger is better than older, pretty is better than ugly, TV is better than music, music is better than movies, movies is better than sports, anything is better than politics, and P.S., nothing is better than a dead celebrity.

Dick Stolley, editor of *People* magazine on choosing whose face to put on the cover each week

Hollywood reporters, all day long, they lie in the sun, and when the sun goes down, they lie some more.

Frank Sinatra

Has any reader ever found perfect accuracy in the newspaper account of any event of which he himself had inside knowledge?

E.V. Lucas

The paper had over a million readers, many of whom could read.

Louella Parsons

Louella Parsons would sit at her telephone all night long, if necessary, interpreting the denials of those she was interrogating as the great horned owl interprets the squeaking of mice.

Paul O'Neil

Interviewing celebrities is just a step above calling the morgue.

Garrison Keiller

An interview for Alfred Hitchcock was like a living autopsy.

Alexander Walker

Interviewing Warren Beatty is like asking a hemophiliac for a pint of blood.

Rex Reed

I don't like giving interviews. I've never heard anything that came out of my mouth that sounded interesting.

Adam Sandler

Someone once said interviews are like thumbprints on your windpipe. That's kinda how I feel.

Johnny Depp

I'm not great on interviews. I'm really not. I just hate
boring people... Somebody comes here and expects
some terrific quote or overview of the world. Like, is
Armageddon about to come and if so will it be before
or after dinner?

Woody Allen

I always give interviews. If the *Poultry Farmers'
Weekly Gazette* rings me up, I'm delighted to be
asked my opinion.

Michael Caine

–Mr Wilder! It's Derek Malcolm from the *Guardian*.
I'm here for the interview.
[from the bathroom]–Come in, come in! I can deal
with two shits at a time.

Derek Malcolm and Billy Wilder

An actor who I won't name says that whenever an
interviewer asks him what has been the low point of
his life, he likes to answer, "This interview."

Peter Finch

When someone says, "That's a good question," he
never has a good answer.

Truman Capote

I've never won an interview yet.

Phil Silvers

Nothing conceals one's real self better than an interview, except more interviews.

Barry Pain

I improve on misquotation.

Cary Grant

Every actor in his heart believes everything bad that's printed about him.

Orson Welles

I never looked through a keyhole without finding someone was looking back.

Judy Garland on lack of privacy

FILM CRITICS

Reviewing films is for women and fairies.

Harold Ross

The main qualities of a successful film critic are good typing skills, firm gluteal muscles, and the ability to sleep with one's eyes open.

Duane Byrge

What then is the function of the film critic? Precisely to interpret the audio-visual electronic image and fragmentize individual coercive response against a background of selective subjectivity. He can do this either standing up or sitting.

Woody Allen

Don't pay any attention to the critics; don't even
ignore them.

Sam Goldwyn

Fuck the critics. They're like eunuchs. They can tell
you how to do it, but they can't do it themselves.

Harry Cohn

I'm too rich to care what the critics say.

Mel Gibson

I wouldn't take the advice of a lot of so-called critics
on how to shoot a close-up of a teapot.

David Lean

An actor can remember his briefest notice well into
senescence and long after he has forgotten his phone
number and where he lives.

Jean Kerr

They're not critics, they're success-haters.

Tim Rice

A critic is a newspaper man whose sweetheart ran
away with an actor.

Walter Winchell

It's wonderful when it isn't you.

John Gielgud on reading bad reviews

One finds that as the years go by one has already reviewed, under another title, almost every new film one sees.

Dwight MacDonald

–I think the picture stinks.
–Who the hell are you to think the picture stinks?
–Who the hell do you have to be to think the picture stinks?

Oscar Levant and Darryl F. Zanuck

Intellectually, I'd like to think of critics as running-dog conspirators against the institutions of art. But they're just jack-offs like the rest of us.

David Mamet

Who are the critics, anyway? Just a bunch of Joes with passes.

Variety

–What do you think of critics?
–They're very noisy at night. You can't sleep in the country because of them.
–No, I said critics, not crickets.
–Oh, critics! What good are they? They can't make music with their hind legs.

Carl Reiner and Mel Brooks

FILM REVIEWS

–What did you think of Titanic?

–I'd rather have been on it.

Interviewer and Miles Kruger

In Titanic, James Cameron had to invent a Romeo-and-Juliet-style fictional couple to heat up what was a real-life catastrophe. This seems a tiny bit like giving Anne Frank a wacky best friend, to perk up the attic.

Libby Gelman-Waxner

Many of the characters in Titanic are clichés of such purity they ought to be exhibited in film schools as examples of how not to write for the screen.

Kenneth Turan

The Hindenburg manages to make one of the century's most sensational real-life catastrophes seem roughly as terrifying as a stubbed toe.

Frank Rich

Was it Rodin who said that he sculpted with his penis? The message of Shakespeare in Love is that Shakespeare wrote with his. Gwyneth, bed, nipples, love, moan, morning, manuscript. Magic. No ink. No pen. Nothing. Just Gwyneth in his arms and that's *Romeo and Juliet* completed.

Howard Jacobson

To go or not to go, strewth, that is the question.

Time Out on Hamlet starring Mel Gibson

Hamlet is a great story. It's got some great things in it. I mean, there's something like eight violent deaths.

Mel Gibson

Mel Gibson's enunciation in Hamlet had the unreal clarity of a speaking clock.

The Times

R2D2's voice in Star Wars anticipates, with uncanny accuracy, the speed-dial function of a touch-tone phone.

Mark Steyn

Star Wars: The Phantom Menace is easily consumable eye-candy that contains no nutrients for the heart or mind.

Variety

Spice World—a thinly disguised imitation of A Hard Day's Night with a worse script and more bras.

Luis Bernabe

South Park—Bigger, Longer & Uncut: It isn't anarchic, it's something much more offensive —it's cute.

Sydney Morning Herald

Resurrection Man leaves you with the feeling of
having been on an occasionally unguided tour
of an abattoir.

Richard Falcon

9½ Weeks and Two Moon Junction put the rot back
into erotica.

Christopher Tookey

Watching The Stud is rather like being buried alive
in a coffin stuffed with back numbers of *Men Only*.

Alan Brien

The two most important words in Last Tango in Paris
are 'tango' and 'Paris,' both of which are regarded
as sophisticated and adult. Last Hokey-Cokey in
Macclesfield wouldn't be the same at all.

Mark Steyn

Forrest Gump is roughly as truthful about the world
of intellectual handicap as The Little Mermaid is
about fish.

Christopher Tookey

Independence Day: I like it. We won. The end.

Senator Bob Dole

Watching Manhattan, it almost makes you forget all
the dog poo on the streets.

Maureen Stapleton

Pulp Fiction sets a precedent as the very first Disney film to feature anal rape.

Jeff Dawson

The Blue Lagoon is a Sunday school fairy tale, as hygienically sanitized as a Hilton Hotel lavatory seat.

The Times

The Incredible Sarah is a job lot of obligatory Hollywood platitudes strung together with all the skill of Captain Hook trying to thread a needle.

Benny Green

Lonesome Cowboy is Andy Warhol's best movie to date, which is like saying a 3-year-old has graduated from smearing faeces on the wall to the occasional use of finger-paints.

Variety

When Ben Stiller got his penis caught in the zipper of his polyster tuxedo pants, in close-up, I'm telling you, for the first time ever I thought of the words Jerry Lewis and nuance in the same sentence.

Libby Gelman-Waxner on There's Something About Mary

The re-enactment of the shower scene in Psycho ends with Anne Heche collapsing over the side of the bath with her pert bottom sticking up in the air like a novelty bike-rest.

Mark Steyn on Psycho directed by Gus Van Sant

Films based on video games are about as worthwhile as novels written by supermodels.

Daily Telegraph on **Wing Commander**

Music you can see and pictures you can hear.

Walt Disney on Fantasia

Ken Russell casts himself in the title role of his own film, The Secret Life of Arnold Bax, and gives a portrayal so dire that I suspect he may have had to perform sexual favors for himself on the casting couch in order to get the part.

Victor Lewis-Smith

Another Woman is a feel-good movie only in the sense that you feel much better when you stop watching it.

Simon Rose

Two jokes I heard in Israel: 1) There's no business like Shoah business. 2) Do you know why Hitler killed himself? He got his gas bill. Are these jokes revolting? They may or may not be, but they are legitimate attempts to use a dramatic form (the joke) to address the insoluble and oppressive phenomenon of genocide. Schindler's List, on the other hand, is an exploitation film.

David Mamet

Leave it to Steven Spielberg to make a feel-good movie entertainment about the ultimate feel-bad experience. And don't worry about dinner afterwards - Schindler's List is a tasteful movie.

> J. Hoberman

Schindler's List is about success. It is not about the Holocaust. The Holocaust is about 6 million people who get killed. Schindler's List was about 600 people who don't.

> Stanley Kubrick

Mrs Miniver is an exemplary propaganda film for the German film industry to copy.

> Paul Joseph Goebbels

The Sound of Mucus.

> Pauline Kael on The Sound of Music

Notting Hill: Romantic world view with heavy pagan elements and amoral ending. 41 obscenities, 12 profanities plus many sexual references. EXTREME CAUTION.

> Crosswalk. com, US website for Christians

One might have said that the plot of Car Trouble would have been improved by the introduction of an ax-wielding maniac, except that there already is an ax-wielding maniac and he doesn't improve it at all.

> *Time Out*

Jack Frost stars Michael Keaton as a rock musician
who dies and is reincarnated as a snowman. It
should never have been made as a movie, it should
have been made as an episode of Ricki Lake, entitled,
"My Daddy's Nose is a Cork."

Neil LaBute

Parting Shots is essentially the equivalent of vanity
publishing: a film directed by Michael Winner,
produced by Michael Winner, written by Michael
Winner, edited by Michael Winner, and made for
Michael Winner to watch, perhaps in company
with Michael Winner's current girlfriend.

Mark Steyn

I would like to recommend Random Harvest to those
who can stay interested in Ronald Colman's amnesia
for two hours and who could with pleasure eat a
bowl of Yardley's shaving soap for breakfast.

James Agee

Heaven's Gate is the most scandalous cinematic waste
I have ever seen, and remember, I've seen Paint Your
Wagon.

Roger Ebert

A film so dire it deserves to be reviewed in the
obituary column.

Laura Baum on Heaven's Gate

I remember arriving on the set of Heaven's Gate when they were shooting a scene that in the script was described as "Averell passes the cockfight on the way to the bar." When I got there, they were on the third week of shooting the cockfight, which really says it all.

John Hurt

Health easily won this year's Listerine Prize for lousy word of mouth.

Charles Champlin

No matter where you come in during the running of Beat the Devil, you seem to have missed at least half the picture.

Harry Kurnitz

The Boys in the Band: How very unlike the home life of our own dear queens.

Anon

Mary Poppins is unsupercalifragilisticexpialidocious.
Gilbert Adair

Love Story: Die, witch! Die!

Joe Queenan

Stunts: less than cunning.

Roger Parsons

Matador: Picador and leave.

Christopher Tookey

Divorce His, Divorce Hers: All the joy of standing by at an autopsy.

Variety

One is reminded of a British critic's comment on Mary of Scotland: "the inaccuracies must have involved tremendous research."

Robert Stebbins on Lost Horizon

What is wrong with a little incest? It is both handy and cheap.

James Agate on The Barretts of Wimpole Street

The only thing Oliver Stone got right in JFK was the date of Kennedy's death.

Gerald Posner

They only got two things right in Lawrence of Arabia: the camels and the sand.

Lowell Thomas

The censors say you have to be 18 to see Friday The 13th: The Final Chapter. I would suggest you merely have to be daft.

Sunday Times

The camerawork showed all the mobility of a concrete fire hydrant caught in a winter freeze.

Paul D. Zimmermann on The Cocoanuts

Did you ever try to shoot swallows in a cyclone? It's easy compared to reviewing a Marx Brothers film.

Rob Wagner

CENSORSHIP

If they didn't show it on the screen, most people would never know about oral sex.

Mary Whitehouse

There is no preacher who can't get at least three rousing sermons annually out of Hollywood.

Nunnally Johnson

A sermon against the evils of promiscuous sex indulgence can send a congregation home to masturbate as quickly as a reading from *Fanny Hill*.

Ben Hecht

–Will you be taking your clothes off in the new film?
–Absolutely, I'll find some excuse.

Reporter and Helen Mirren

Nudity is a profound ice-breaker.

Tallulah Bankhead

Nude scenes? I wouldn't take off my clothes. There's enough violence in the world.

Carol Burnett

This isn't an X-rated body. This is a PG body.

Mariel Hemingway

I'm not prudish about exposing my body. I'm much more uptight about exposing my mind to the wrong people.

Lauren Hutton

When they said that tickets for Hair were $10 apiece, I went into the bathroom, took off my clothes and looked in the mirror for ten minutes and said, "It isn't worth it."

Groucho Marx

I don't do dirty material. I guess I'm a prude at heart. Even if I'm home alone, I close the door when I go to the bathroom.

George Burns

Pubic hair is no substitute for wit.

J.B. Priestley

When Demi Moore did a striptease on the David Letterman Show she said she wasn't doing it for the guys but to prove that "feminism can still be feminine." That's akin to a turkey stuffing sage and onion stuffing up its arse to prove it's not oppressed by Christmas.

Ben Elton

It'a a new low for actresses when you have to wonder what's between her ears instead of her legs.

Katharine Hepburn on Sharon Stone

207

Sharon Stone famously declared that "Hollywood is frightened of anyone who has a brain and a vagina" —from the lofty perch she reached solely by displaying only one of these attributes to the world.

> Boyd Farrow

Sharon Stone and Demi Moore both exist to discuss how they want to stretch as artists while holding their hands over their breasts on the cover of *Vanity Fair*.

> Libby Gelman-Waxner

When you get the personality, you don't need the nudity.

> Mae West

Real pornography is movies starring Doris Day.

> Al Alvarez

We have Viagra. Why should it be that you are allowed to be chemically aroused but not visually?

> James Ferman

Why is everyone in an adult movie a porn star? How come we never hear about any porn co-stars? Where are the porn character-actors? Where are the porn extras? Are you automatically a star when you're in a porn movie?

> Jay Leno

No one's ever held up a bank with a dildo.

> Lenny Bruce

Soft-core porn is where you pretend to have sex but really you're not—like the Clintons.

Jay Leno

If you suck a woman's breast, it's rated X. If you cut it off, it gets an R.

Jack Nicholson

I would rather pretend to be having an orgasm than pretend someone's stabbing me a thousand times. It's a more pleasant image.

Heather Graham

I'm a student of violence because I'm a student of the human heart.

Sam Peckinpah

I will trade you forty gorgeous Hawaiian sunsets for one good sock in the jaw.

Cecil B. De Mille

Reservoir Dogs is not that violent, it's intense.

Quentin Tarantino

Seeing Bambi's mum get killed is probably more frightening than anything in Reservoir Dogs.

Quentin Tarantino

I saw Reservoir Dogs. It would have gone down well with the Waffen SS.

Ken Russell

HOLLYWOOD WIT

A far more disturbing spectacle than the cartoonish-
ly violent Pulp Fiction, was the director's cartoonish
dancing at the MTV party in Cannes.

Boyd Farrow

A slasher film by Martin Scorsese is still a slasher
film.

Dave Kehr on Cape Fear

I've always fancied myself with a gun in my hand,
but I'm pathologically frightened of loud bangs.

Hugh Grant

Thanks to the movies, real gunfire has always
sounded unreal to me, even when being fired at.

Peter Ustinov

One line from Lock, Stock and Two Smoking Barrels
plays like a credo of the Hollywood film industry
right now. After a hail of bullets, we hear a terrified
bloke pleading, "Could everyone of you stop
getting shot?"

Marion Hart

American society is a society of revenge. The scientist
in our culture is unknown; Billy the Kid is not.

Oliver Stone

A censor is a man who knows more than he thinks
you ought to.

Laurence Peter

Thirty or so people were killed in The Godfather but
the only complaints we got were over the horse's
head. "You killed a living animal!" they cried. Not I.
The horse was killed by the dog food companies to
feed your little poodles.

Francis Coppola

I have always thought that in the motion picture
business the real violence was not what people do on
the screen, but what we do to raise the money.

David Mamet

We are paid to have dirty minds.

John Trevelyan, censor

Belief in Hollywood's influence is rather like the
belief in life after death. Most of us would like to be
able to prove it but the evidence is inconclusive.

Lloyd Mason

I don't think that guys really want to hit people; they
just want to see movies about hitting people. And
women don't want equal pay and self-esteem; we
want to see BRAD PITT WEARING HIS PANTS 15
INCHES BELOW HIS BELLY BUTTON.

Libby Gelman-Waxner

There is no such thing as a dirty theme. There are
only dirty writers.

George Jean Nathan

211

If Ernest Lehman had written The Sound of Music a little dirtier, and if he had written Who's Afraid of Virginia Woolf? a little cleaner, he would never have the money that he has today.

I.A.L Diamond

I believe in censorship. After all, I made a fortune out of it.

Mae West

Mae West's I'm No Angel has no more pretence at romance than a stud farm.

Code of Recommendation Report, 1933

We approached the Production Code Administration to adapt Double Indemnity and were sent one of those things that begin UNDER NO CIRCUMSTANCES and wind up WAY, SHAPE OR FORM.

James M. Cain

You go in to The Hays Office with your dreams and you come out with the Parent-Teachers' Association.

Raymond Chandler

I resigned my job as a censor. I've got nothing against sex, it's a marvelous human activity, but it was watching others do it all the time that got me down.

John Trevelyan

SUCCESS & FAILURE

When Kipling said treat failure and success the same,
they are both imposters, he could not have been
living in Hollywood.

Lily Tomlin

Our town worships success, the bitch goddess whose
smile hides a taste for blood.

Hedda Hopper

Nobody is allowed to fail within a two-mile radius of
the Beverly Hills Hotel.

Gore Vidal

When things are going well in Hollywood, it's
absolutely delightful, if you like sycophancy.

Hugh Grant

The qualities that make people a success in
Hollywood and the way they get to the top are
exactly the same as they are for any job.

Cornel Wilde

Success to me is having ten honeydew melons, and
eating only the top half of each one.

Barbra Streisand

An actor's success has the life expectancy of a small
boy about to look into a gas tank with a lighted
match.

Fred Allen

213

Eighty per cent of success is showing up.

Woody Allen

The toughest thing about success is that you've got to keep on being a success.

Irving Berlin

The worst thing about having success is trying to find someone who is happy for you.

Bette Midler

In Hollywood, after you get a little success, the next thing you usually get is a divorce.

Dan Dailey

I don't try to guess what a million people will like. It's hard enough to know what I like.

John Huston

You know you're successful when they make porno versions of your films. They remade Edward Scissorhands as Edward Penis-hands.

Tim Burton

There is no formula for success. But there is a formula for failure, and that is trying to please everybody.

Nicholas Ray

Hollywood sets out to give the people what they want. The most horrifying thing is what people do want.

Martin Lane

Don't give the public what they want. Give them
something better.

"Roxy" Rothafel

You're better off investing in instant scratch cards
than film. At least you'll have the pleasure of doing
the scratching.

David Williams

Nothing is as cheap as a hit, no matter how much it
cost.

Walter Wanger

Five good scenes, and don't annoy the audience, and
it'll be a good picture.

Howard Hawkes

You can seduce a man's wife here, attack his
daughter and wipe your hands on his canary bird,
but if you don't like his movie, you're dead.

Josef von Sternberg

Tell me how did you love my picture?

Sam Goldwyn

Failure has a thousand explanations. Success doesn't
need one.

Alec Guinness

Can you root for the hero and heroine? Can you boo the villain? Is the action fast and furious? If these questions can be answered yes, grab the idea and get into production.

Alan Ladd Jr

–If a picture is great, I sit still. If a picture is good, I move just a little. But if a picture stinks, my ass squirms all over the place.
–Just imagine, the whole world wired to Harry Cohn's ass.

Harry Cohn and Herman Mankiewicz

After the poor reviews for Kiss Me, Stupid, my esteemed writing partner, Iz Diamond, and I, sat and stared at each for 12 weeks. We were like parents who had produced a two-headed child and don't dare to have sex again.

Billy Wilder

You can't go around the theaters handing out cards saying, "It isn't my fault." You go on to the next one.

Preston Sturges

Hollywood is like a bird dog. When things are going badly, it tenses and sniffs at you. It scrapes away at the camouflage. It knows.

David Niven

Being a failure in Hollywood is like starving to death outside a banquet hall with the smells of filet mignon driving you crazy.

Johnny Hyde

I have always been more afraid of pretentiousness than failure.

Billy Wilder

You make a hit film the same way you make a flop.

Robert De Niro

It is not enough that my film succeeds, yours must fail.

Hollywood axiom

Hollywood is a town that doesn't just want you to fail, it wants you to die.

David Geffen

What makes a movie a hit is not the advertising and not the star but this: word of mouth.

William Goldman

Damn word of mouth. There's no way to stop it.

Leonard Goldberg, producer

AWARDS

Welcome to the Academy Awards, or as it's known in my house, Passover.

Bob Hope presenting the Oscars, 1978

Two hours of sparkling entertainment packed into a
four-hour show.

Johnny Carson

The Oscars are like pornography–enticing in
prospect, then boring as hell.

David Hare

I'd rather watch old Doris Day movies than the Oscars.
Orson Welles

You know you're entering new territory when you
realize your outfit cost more than your film.
Jessica Wu, winner of the Oscar for Best Documentary Short,
1998

Here comes Ashley Judd in her no-yeast-infection-
here Oscar gown...

Libby Gelman-Waxner

Working out the seating arrangement is tricky.
Obviously, you're going to put Jack Nicholson in a
great seat, and a facially obscure person in a less
visible seat.

Gil Cates, producer of the Academy Awards
ceremony show

You stars can't take anything for granted. The only
person guaranteed to wake up with a statue
tomorrow is Tipper Gore.

Billy Crystal compering the Oscars show

Ladies and Gentlemen, please welcome Susan
Sarandon and Tim Robbins. Pay attention, I'm
sure they're pissed off about something.

David Letterman, 1993

In the biz, an Oscar is better than sex.

Richard Corliss

Hugh Hudson, Steven Spielberg and Louis Malle are
all better directors than Warren Beatty. Beatty's
Oscar for best director for Reds was the Academy's
acknowledgement that a gorgeous actor, a pretty
boy, could raise $50 million to make that
picture...that lumbering picture.

David Puttnam

The Oscar seems to have been confused with the
Nobel Peace Prize.

Janet Maslin on the 8 Oscars for Gandhi

I wanted to win the Oscar so that I'd get more scripts
without other actors' coffee-stains on them.

Michael Caine

I thought I might win for The Apartment but then
Elizabeth Taylor had her tracheotomy.

Shirley MacLaine

Helen Hunt won the Oscar by weighing less than the
statuette itself.

Libby Gelman-Waxner

I'd never work again for an Oscar-winner who is shorter than the statue.

Larry Gelbart on Dustin Hoffman

I have, a few times, been mistaken for Meryl Streep. Except at Oscar time.

Glenn Close

Dustin Hoffman reached his peak ten years ago. His Academy Award nomination for Wag the Dog is what we in the business call a mercy fuck.

Bill Murray

Just remember, if you thank a long list of people, 4 will be very happy but 99 million will be bored and go to the refrigerator.

Gil Cates, pep-talk to Oscar nominees

Oscar winners' speeches should be limited to one minute, during which they are required by law to thank their cosmetic surgeon and point out—with visual aids—their most recent nips, tucks and enlargements.

Denis Leary

I would like to thank all those people who were happy to bankroll the film as long as I wasn't in it.

Geoffrey Rush accepting Best Actor Oscar for Shine

We want to thank all of you for watching us congratulate ourselves tonight.

Warren Beatty, 1976

I didn't show up at the awards ceremony to collect
any of my first three Oscars. Once I went fishing,
another time there was a war on, and on another
occasion, I remember, I was suddenly taken drunk.

John Ford

The only thing worse than not being nominated
would have been to be nominated and then losing to
Cher. That would have been embarrassing.

Lillian Gish

–What does an Oscar mean?
–Put it this way, Ellen, when you die, the newspaper
obituaries will say, "The Academy Award-winning
actress Ellen Burstyn died today."

Ellen Burstyn and Walter Matthau

Awards? Who needs awards? Best Fascist Director:
Adolf Hitler.

Woody Allen

I don't care what they say to the press, I've never
met an actor in my life who doesn't have an accept-
ance speech going through his head every day.

Jane Fonda

I'll never forget the night I brought my Oscar home
and Tony, my husband, took one look at it and I
knew my marriage was over.

Shelley Winters

I would like to believe in God in order to thank him, but I just believe in Billy Wilder, so...thank you, Mr Wilder.

Fernando Trueba accepting an Oscar, 1994

Nothing would disgust me more, morally, than receiving an Oscar.

Luis Buñuel

–Is there any award left for you to win?
–There's still Crufts.

Reporter and Judi Dench

Academy Awards are like orgasms—only a few of us know the feeling of having had multiple ones.

John Huston, winner of 2 Oscars, 1948

I did not expect this. Actually, I did. But not for another 25 years.

Frederico Fellini accepting an Honorary Oscar, 1992

You should always be surprised by awards and prizes, since you're always surprised when you don't get them.

Edward Albee

Awards are like hemorrhoids; in the end every asshole gets one.

Frederic Raphael

THE LIFESTYLE

FILM FESTIVALS

There is only one reason why anyone goes away to a film festival and that is to cheat on their partner.

Laura Baum

Cannes is where you lie on the beach and stare at the stars—or vice versa.

Rex Reed

Cannes is a film festival in the way that Christmas is a religious festival.

Penelope Houston

In a few days in Cannes you bump into every asshole you've been carefully avoiding all year.

Roman Polanski

Look at all the film buyers and sellers in Cannes any year and you're basically looking at a lot of shoe-salesmen working out whether it should be sneakers or lace-ups next year.

David Hemmings

A sandwich and a Coke cost more on the Croisette than the budget for any European film showing there.

Boyd Farrow

The Sundance Film Festival: an awful lot of rich kids with trust funds making films about poor people.

Unnamed screenwriter

The only problem I have with film festivals are the films.

                                                        Duane Byrge

PARTIES

A gathering held to enable two hundred people to talk about themselves at the same time. The man who remains after the liquor has gone is the host.

                                                        Fred Allen

Parties in Hollywood are lush, and so are most of the guests.

                                                        Groucho Marx

It's just as important to see which party you don't get invited to. It's like a court, but not King Arthur's— more like Richard III's.

                                                        Michael Caine

There are people in Bel Air and Beverly Hills, who when they aren't invited to an A-list party, turn out all their lights so their neighbors won't know they're not at that party.

                                                        Joyce Haber

Hollywood parties? In the old days, if you didn't take the young lady on your right upstairs between the soup and the entrée, you were considered a homosexual.

                                                        Walter Wanger

At my first party there (given for me), I overheard someone say, "He's the guest of honor? Who the fuck is he?" That brought me down to earth.

Michael Caine

It's impossible to take a piss at a Hollywood bash. There are six people in every bathroom at every party. You have to pretend you want to do drugs just to get into the bathroom.

Joel Silver

I once took Elsa Maxwell to a masquerade party. At the stroke of midnight, I ripped off her mask and discovered I had beheaded her.

Oscar Levant

I made appearances at cocktail parties in Florida for $500 a pop, pretending to be an old friend of the host.

Mickey Rooney

Everyone goes home early. 11 o'clock, that's when everyone starts moving. Two reasons: 1) because you have to get up in the morning to work; and 2) if you're out of work you have to look as though you have got to get up.

Michael Caine

There was more good acting at Hollywood parties than ever appeared on the screen.

Bette Davis

226

All social life now is charity fund-raisers. I get 15 letters a day for everything from Yugoslavian dog illnesses to marathon-runner's nipple diseases.

Angelica Huston, 1998

Hollywood parties are an excuse for rich folk to have fun and not feel guilty about it by throwing a few crumbs at the poor.

Dan Lubeck

DRINK

The trouble with the world is that everybody in it is about three drinks behind.

Humphrey Bogart

I drink to forget I drink.

Dean Martin

The best research for playing a drunk is being a British actor for twenty years.

Michael Caine

Arthur Hornblow not only knows what year the wine was made but he can tell you who stamped on the grapes.

Edith Gwynn

My main ambition as a gardener is to water my orange trees with gin, then all I have to do is squeeze the juice into a glass.

W.C. Fields

–Would you like some water with your whisky?
–I have troubles enough without adding to them.

John Barrymore and W.C. Fields

Pour him outta here.

Mae West on W.C. Fields

It's hard to tell where Hollywood ends and the DTs begin.

W.C. Fields

The insurance company doctor has refused to renew my health policy. The nefarious quack claims he found urine in my whisky.

W.C. Fields

–Bill always travels with two wardrobe trunks, one for clothes and one for gin.
–That's a lie. I have gin in both trunks.

Bill Grady and W.C. Fields

The only cure for a real hangover is death.

Robert Benchley

I gave up drinking after I realized that English had become my second language after slurring.

Billy Connolly

I never should have switched from Scotch to
Martinis.

Humphrey Bogart, his last words

ADDICTIONS

Hollywood is divided into two groups. Those who do
cocaine and those who don't.

Terence Young

–What was the budget for the movie?
–I'll tell you what the cocaine budget was: $750,000.
–Well, it's all up there on the screen.

Michael Caine and unnamed producer

A great many people in Los Angeles are on strict
diets that restrict their intake of synthetic foods.
The reason for this appears to be a widely-held
belief that organically grown fruit and vegetables
make the cocaine work faster.

Fran Lebowitz

Cocaine is God's way of letting you know you make
too much money.

Robin Williams

The reason I don't do drugs is that I would like them
too much.

Ben Stiller

The worst drug of today is not smack or pot—it's refined sugar.

George Hamilton

My weakness is wearing too much leopard print.

Jackie Collins

Celebrity is as addictive and destructive as any drink and I am a recovering celebrity.

Barry Manilow

The problem with people who have no vices is that generally you can be pretty sure they're going to have some pretty annoying virtues.

Elizabeth Taylor

The most expensive habit in the world is celluloid, not heroin, and I need a fix every few years.

Steven Spielberg

I'm for anything that gets you through the night, be it prayer, tranquilizers or a bottle of Jack Daniels.

Frank Sinatra

PSYCHOANALYSIS

Hollywood is the greatest boon to psychiatrists since sex.

Nunnally Johnson

In Hollywood, everyone goes to a therapist, is a therapist, or is a therapist going to a therapist.

Truman Capote

I am thinking of going to a clinic in La Jolla where they take in decayed personalities and try to find out if it is any use letting them live.

Raymond Chandler

I once asked Woody Allen how his psychoanalysis was going after 25 years. He said, "Slowly."

John Cleese

Woody Allen didn't even buy sheets without talking to his psychiatrist. I know that several sessions went into his switch from polyester-satin to cotton.

Mia Farrow

–Does psychoanalysis help your constipation?
–No, but now I understand why I have constipation.

George Gershwin and Oscar Levant

Tell us your phobias and we will tell you what you are afraid of.

Robert Benchley

I made a comment to a newspaper about therapists saying that people should not become dependent on them and it got printed as, "The rapists say..."

Oscar Levant

My psychiatrist once said to me, "Maybe life isn't for everyone."

Oscar Levant

I told my psychiatrist that everyone hates me. He said I was being ridiculous—everyone hasn't met me yet.

Rodney Dangerfield

It would be proper to put the name of my analyst in the credits of my films.

Bernardo Bertolucci

I've never been through psychoanalysis. I solve my problems with the pictures I make.

Steven Spielberg

My mom had the breakdown for the family, and I went into therapy for all of us.

Carrie Fisher

Tell your troubles to a bartender—who ever heard of a shrink giving you one on the house?

Jackie Gleason

Couches are for one thing only.

John Wayne

MONEY

Everybody does it for the money.

David Thomson

Long ago, Hollywood decided that the way to keep people quiet is to overpay them.

William Goldman

Hollywood money is something you throw off the ends of trains.

Charles MacArthur

A man can make more money with less effort in the movies than in any other profession.

George Sanders

You get paid the same for a bad film as you do for a good one.

Michael Caine

Never in my life have I seen so many unhappy men making $100,000 a year.

Walter Wanger, 1940

Having a lot of money is like eating popcorn. It fills you up but it isn't very satisfying.

Ted Turner

You can't eat more than one pastrami-on-rye sand-wich at a time.

Barbra Streisand

Ma wished me luck with my movie and said, "Son, I hope it makes a million." "But, Ma," I said, "it cost 22 million to make."

Mel Brooks

Hollywood money is like so much congealed snow. It goes so fast it melts in your hand.

Dorothy Parker

If it's a good script I'll do it. And if it's a bad script, and they pay me enough, I'll do it.

George Burns

People will swim through shit if you put a few bob in it.

Peter Sellers

I notice that the width of a Hollywood smile in my direction is commensurate with how much my last picture grossed.

Marlon Brando

I don't mind that I'm fat. You still get the same money.

Marlon Brando

I asked Marlon Brando why he hadn't read the script of Superman and he said, "Well, they pay me a lot of money to do this, and if I read it, I might not want to do it, and I really need the money."

Terence Stamp

A million dollars isn't what it used to be.

Howard Hughes, 1937

Marlon Brando got, for an aggregate of 20 minutes on the screen in Superman and Apocalypse Now, more money than Clark Gable got for 20 years at MGM.

Billy Wilder

Judy Garland was the lowest paid star in The Wizard of Oz. Only Toto got paid less.

James Mason

The budget for Apocalypse Now was over $25 million. For that sort of money, we could have invaded somewhere.

Clint Eastwood, 1980

The three watershed movies in my career—Lethal Weapon, 48 HRS, and Commando—were all made for about $15 million. That's the catering budget on a film that I make today.

Joel Silver, 1991

Money gets you laid.

Jack Nicholson

The bigger their budgets, the bigger their heads. It's egonomics.

Brad Lucas

Harry Warner bled whenever he read the budget of a movie.

Wilson Mizner

They spent $60,000 on The Blair Witch Project. What did they spend the money on?

David Letterman

Film profit is like the horizon. It always recedes as you get closer.

Joel Silver

Money is power. And the more money you make, the more power you have. People are going to take your opinion a lot more seriously if they pay you more money, because they can't think of themselves as having made a mistake.

Paul Schrader

Money makes even bastards legitimate.

Billy Wilder

The only reason to have money is to tell any sonovabitch in the world to go to hell.

Humphrey Bogart

I am in an age group where it is rude to discuss money, and now it is all anyone cares about.

Jack Nicholson

If someone's dumb enough to offer me a million dollars to make a picture, I am certainly not dumb enough to turn it down.

Elizabeth Taylor

Ah, well, that's another Matisse.

**Jack Nicholson, finishing a week's work
as the Joker in Batman**

Today, a million dollars is what you pay a star you
don't want.

William Goldman, 1984

I'd have worked for less, but nobody asked me.

Lynn Fontanne

Cary Grant is so rich he could, if he wanted to, join
NATO.

***Time* magazine, 1966**

—In one year that stinker's got through $100,000 of
my money.
—Tell me, darling, is the screwing you're getting worth
the screwing you're getting?

Unnamed actress and Barbara Stanwyck

I was like a kept woman during my twenty-one years
at MGM. You didn't need to carry money. Your face
was your credit card—all over the world.

Walter Pidgeon

I have no bad feelings about actors getting $20
million a picture or more. They won't give you a
dime in this town unless you can make them a
dollar. No producer is going to give anybody $20
million if he doesn't think he's going to make
much more.

Rod Steiger

I made my first million dollars the old fashioned
way: I made a hundred million for somebody else.

Roseanne

However toplofty and idealistic a man may be, he
can always rationalize his right to earn money.

Raymond Chandler

–Is it true you spent more than $50,000 on hookers?
–It does add up, doesn't it?

Reporter and Charlie Sheen

I must have gone through $10 million during my
career. Part of the loot went for gambling, part for
horses and part for women. The rest I spent foolishly.

George Raft

I've done the most unutterable rubbish, all because
of money. I didn't need it...the lure of the zeros was
simply too great.

Richard Burton

Money doesn't buy happiness. But happiness isn't
everything.

Jean Seberg

It's not that it's so good with money, but that it's so
bad without it.

George Sanders

I'm sorry, my good fellow, but all my money is tied up in currency.

W.C. Fields refusing a handout to a beggar

I only give to one charity: the F.E.B.F (Fuck Everybody But Fields).

W.C. Fields

Billy Connolly gives away money as silently as a waiter falling down a flight of stairs with a tray of glasses.

Anon

I've never been poor, only broke. Being poor is a frame of mind. Being broke is only a temporary situation.

Mike Todd

I'm not mean, I'm Scottish.

Sean Connery

We couldn't afford a proper bath. We just had a pan of water and we'd wash down as far as possible and we'd wash up as far as possible. Then, when somebody'd clear the room, we'd wash possible.

Dolly Parton

Compassion is a luxury of the affluent.

Tony Randall

My worst fault is my belief that if you put bills unopened behind a picture frame, there is no need to pay them.

Hermione Gingold

One of my first jobs, before I became a journalist,
was with a firm which collected bad debts; well,
have you ever heard of a good debt?

Ring Lardner

Any man who has $10,000 left when he dies is a
failure.

Errol Flynn

Money doesn't make you happy. I have $50 million
but I was just as happy when I had $48 million.

Arnold Schwarzenegger

I don't worry about money as long as I can reconcile
my net income with my gross habits.

Errol Flynn

I'm not interested in money. I only want to be
wonderful.

Marilyn Monroe

MOVIES: ART OR BUSINESS?

You want art? Buy a Picasso.

Michael Winner

In Hollywood, art is the synonym for bankruptcy.

Ben Hecht

I don't think I've ever seen a great film. Not in the
sense that Ludwig's 5th or Leo's *War and Peace* are
great.

Robert Bolt

One of the joys of going to the movies was that it was trashy, and we should never lose that.

Oliver Stone

Art? Forget it. I've got an agent, a lawyer, a public-relations firm, a business manager, an ex-wife, two kids and a girlfriend to support. I also love fresh broiled Maine lobster.

George Peppard

It's no use asking me to talk about art, I make pictures to pay the rent.

John Ford

We make movies, American movies. Leave the films to the French.

Sam Shephard

In America it is considered a lot more important to be a great Batman that a great Hamlet.

Kevin Kline

I don't make art, I buy it.

Joel Silver

If I ever start talking about "my craft" or "my instrument" you have permission to shoot me point-blank.

Drew Barrymore

Never make an audience think. It always worked for me.

Joe Pasternak

Doing the opposite of what Hollywood would do does not ensure that what you have produced is art. It simply means that what you have produced is three hours long and has Iggy Pop in it.

Tom Shone

Art is for someone to figure out a hundred years from now.

George Lucas

In Hollywood, the executives have Picassos and Chagalls on their walls and would kill to have lunch with Chuck Norris. That's why you have movies like Howard the Duck.

David Steinberg

If Hollywood can package cigarettes and fill them with sawdust, it isn't going to fill them with tobacco.

Robert Mitchum

There aren't any real movie makers any more. The business is run by the cornflakes men and they are only in it for the girls.

Peter O'Toole

Film business? I enjoy the film but the business is shit.

Oliver Stone

Actors are the only kind of merchandise allowed to leave the store at night.

Ava Gardner

The businessmen don't care if you mess your life up,
as long as you don't die during the film.

Richard Pryor

Nobody knows anything.

William Goldman

POLITICS

The politics of Hollywood are horrible—it makes
Washington look like Sesame Street.

Steve Tisch

Politics is for people who are too ugly to get into
show business.

Bill Clinton

Most politicians I put in a class with blackjack
dealers. These characters wouldn't inspire
confidence in the average bail bondsman.

Woody Allen

Old, stupid, bullshit-dressing, pinchy-faced, golfing,
badhair-day people. I can't bear Republicans.

Cher

In politics, nothing succeeds like nothing.

Warren Beatty

Washington comes to Hollywood only when it wants
to raise money or raise hell.

Charlton Heston

I've been married to a communist and a fascist, and neither of them would take out the trash.

Zsa Zsa Gabor

It is getting to be harder and harder to tell government from show business.

Michael J. Rosen

A man who handled the Cuban Missile Crisis—the most dangerous crisis in the 20th century—in the way Kennedy did, deserved an affair with Marilyn Monroe.

George Walden

I'm surprised none of the Kennedys have gone into show business. We have mediocre actors becoming politicians, but we never seem to have politicians turning their deceptive skills to the silver screen. I guess the only fictitious characters they like to portray are themselves.

Truman Capote

I have always liked the Kennedys as politicians. They had such great hair.

Pamela Anderson

Jack Kennedy's murder was one of the two most horrid moments of my life. The other was when I found out there was no Santa Claus.

Tallulah Bankhead

The winner of the presidential pageant will always be the one with the brightest smile and the most hair. It it doubtful if there will be a swimsuit category, but there will never be a bald-headed president again.

Gore Vidal

Politics is supposed to be the second oldest profession. I have come to realize that it bears a very close resemblance to the first.

Ronald Reagan

We elected a President, not a Pope.

Barbra Streisand on the Clinton scandal

There are three times in life when it's useless trying to hold a man to anything he says—when he's madly in love, drunk or running for office.

Robert Mitchum

Warren Beatty says he's thinking of running for President—well, it's someone to carry on the Clinton legacy. Does he have a chance? As long as Brad Pitt stays outta the race.

Jay Leno

One of the most depressing remarks that was made when I first came to the House of Commons was by an MP who said, "What d'you want to come here for? You're famous already."

Glenda Jackson

I would never run for President. Some people have skeletons in their closets, but I have a graveyard.

Sylvester Stallone

–The trouble with England is it's being governed by cunts.
–Quite frankly, old man, there're an awful lot of cunts in England, and they deserve representation.

Rex Harrison and Unnamed Member of Parliament

BELIEFS

Where is Hollywood located? Chiefly between the ears. In that part of the American brain lately vacated by God.

Erica Jong

The movies are a gaudier version of religion.

Ben Hecht

If you had to worship something mortal on earth, I would go and bow twice a day to wherever Laurence Olivier was standing.

Sammy Davis Jr

My religion? I'm a retired Christian.

Peter O'Toole

The trouble with born-again Christians is that they are an even bigger pain the second time around.

Denis Leary

–You could probably convert me because I'm a push-over. And if you make it appealing enough and you promise me some wonderful afterlife with a white robe and wings...I could go for it.
–I can't promise you wings...but I can promise you a wonderful, exciting life.
–One wing?

Woody Allen and Billy Graham, TV interview

–Congratulate me. I've just signed a new 5-year deal at RKO.
–You can't work for RKO. The goddamn place is run by Jews.
–What are you talking about? George Schaefer is the head of RKO and he's a Catholic.
–Catholics, they're the worst kind of Jews.

Gregory La Cava and W.C. Fields

I was banned from the Beverly Hills swimming club because I'm Jewish. "My son's only half Jewish," I told them, "so could he go in up to his waist?"

Groucho Marx

The only advantage I have found to being Jewish is that I can be openly anti-Semitic.

Kirk Douglas

I do benefits for all religions. I'd hate to blow the hereafter on a technicality.

Bob Hope

I've tried Buddhism, Scientology, Numerology, Transcendental Meditation, kabbala, tai-chi, feng shui and Deepak Chopra but I find straight gin works best.

Phyllis Diller

I'm very into Taoism. Ever since I read that book, *The Tao of Pooh*.

Wes Bentley

I knew it was going to be a bad day. My karma ran over my dogma.

Billy Connolly

Everybody should believe in something; I believe I'll have another drink.

Robert Benchley

THE LOOK

SEX APPEAL

I could never understand what Godfrey Tearle saw in
Jill Bennett, until I saw her at the Caprice eating
corn-on-the-cob.

Coral Browne

There are two good reasons why men go to see Jane
Russell. Those are enough.

Howard Hughes

Sometimes the photographers would pose me in a
low-necked nightgown and tell me to bend down and
pick up the pails. They were not shooting the pails.

Jane Russell

Miss Russell's breasts hang over the picture like a
summer thunderstorm spread out over a landscape.

Maryland judge imposing a state ban on The Outlaw

Rita Hayworth danced on to the screen in a flaming
red dress, cut to show a major part of her acting
ability.

Gerald Lieberman

Men like me because I don't wear a brassière.
Women like me because I don't look like a girl who
would steal a husband. At least not for long.

Jean Harlow

Dramatic art in Jayne Mansfield's opinion is
knowing how to fill a sweater.

Bette Davis

With Kathryn Grayson around they didn't need 3-D.

Ava Gardner

Jean Harlow's technique was the gangster's technique
—she toted a breast like a man totes a gun.

Graham Greene

I asked Dylan Thomas why he'd come to Hollywood
and very solemnly he said, "To touch a starlet's tits."
"Okay," I said, "but only one finger."

Shelley Winters

When we started shooting Roman Holiday, Willie Wyler
came up to me and said, "If you don't mind my saying
so, I think you should wear falsies." I said, "I am!"

Audrey Hepburn

In Star Wars, they taped down my breasts because
George Lucas said there are no breasts in space.

Carrie Fisher

The legs aren't so beautiful. I just know what to do
with them.

Marlene Dietrich

I've been getting by for years on what I didn't show
the boys.

Mae West

I will have one of the cleanest obits of any actress. I never did cheesecake like Ann Sheridan or Betty Grable. I just used my hair.

Veronica Lake

Meryl Streep can act Polish or English or Australian but she sure as hell can't act blonde.

Joan Bennett

No one ever sounded as blonde as Marilyn Monroe did.

Billy Wilder

When I first met Zsa Zsa Gabor I saw she was one of those blondes who put on ten years if you take a close look at them.

Marilyn Monroe

I'm not offended by dumb blonde jokes because I know I'm not dumb, and I know I'm not blonde.

Dolly Parton

I've been condemned from more pulpits than Satan.

Brigitte Bardot

At the height of his Bond fame, Sean Connery could have had any woman in the world. And as far as I could see, he often did.

Diana Dors

In Indecent Proposal Demi Moore sells herself to
Robert Redford for a million dollars. That's ludicrous
—I'd shag him for a tenner.

Jo Brand

Who are the guys who you would strip naked to the
waist? Hanks you wouldn't. Harrison Ford, barely.
Jim Carrey, you'd think twice. Travolta, no way. Who
is the guy taking over from Bruce Willis and
Sylvester Stallone? There's no Beefcake left. It's all
Spam.

Brad Lucas

BEAUTY & UGLINESS

The way I look at it, I'm a human being first and
gorgeous second.

Harvey Fierstein

In Hollywood, the women are all peaches. It makes
one long for an apple occasionally.

Somerset Maugham

Great beauties are infrequently great actresses,
simply because they do not need to be.

Garson Kanin

Most beautiful but dumb girls think they are smart
and get away with it, because other people, on the
whole, aren't much smarter.

Louise Brooks

253

Any girl can be glamorous. All you have to do is stand still and look stupid.

Hedy Lamarr

I went to a plastic surgeon for a facelift after a friend said it would be a good idea. The surgeon suggested I change my friend, not my face.

Sally Burton

When they tell me to get my nose fixed I tell 'em to take a hike. I can smell just swell with the one I got.

Robert Mitchum

Years of cosmetic surgery have transformed Michael Jackson into a pubescent Elizabeth Taylor.

Allison Pearson

Joan Rivers's face hasn't just had a lift, it's taken the elevator all the way to the top floor without stopping.

Clive James

After the nuclear holocaust, the only two creatures to survive will be the common cockroach and Cher.

Jan Moir

If Cher has another face-lift she'll be wearing a beard.

Jennifer Saunders

The only parts left of my original body are my elbows.

Phyllis Diller

Gwyneth Paltrow is the only 26-year-old in Hollywood who looks as though she has already had a face-lift.

Julie Burchill

Today, even the screenwriters in Hollywood are getting face-lifts. That's how ageist this town is.

Gil MacIntyre

We always say that these men in Hollywood who want their penises enlarged ought to have their other head examined.

Dr Hunter Wessels, plastic surgeon

Louis B. Mayer once looked at me and said, "You will never get the girl at the end." So I worked on my acting.

Van Heflin

I know one or two actors who are homely enough for it to be assumed that because they look so plain they must be good actors—and they're not.

Peter Ustinov

I was initially passed over for The Accused. They said I didn't look "rape-able" enough.

Jodie Foster

There's a lot of good-looking, well-built guys in this business and most of them couldn't play a corpse.

James Caan

255

Caribbean blue eyes. The knowing mouth. A fine
figure that stops just this side of martial artistry.
These are the anonymous good looks of an
afternoon actor.

Richard Corliss on Alec Baldwin, ex-soap star

Sometimes my face is more beautiful than the leading lady's.

Rosanno Brazzi

"You will have the tallest, darkest leading man in
Hollywood." Those were the first words I heard about
King Kong.

Fay Wray

Alain Delon is beautiful, but so is the Louis XVI
commode I have.

Brigitte Bardot

You think beautiful girls are going to stay in style
forever?

Barbra Streisand

Humphrey Bogart is the ugliest handsome man I've
ever seen.

Lauren Bacall

Utter ugliness like mine is the most attractive. I'm
convinced that a really ugly man, in the end,
seems attractive.

Sammy Davis Jr

VANITY & MODESTY

–I simply can't find the words to tell you how superb
you were.

–Try.

Claire Trevor and Judith Anderson

An actor is a kind of guy who, if you ain't talking
about him, he ain't listening.

Marlon Brando

You can pick out actors by the glazed look that comes
into their eyes when the conversation wanders away
from themselves.

Michael Wilding

The whole motivation for any performer is "Look at
me, Ma."

Lenny Bruce

I'm always acting, even when I'm alone in a room.

Charles Laughton

I like to be introduced as America's foremost actor. It
saves the necessity of further effort.

John Barrymore

Stop, stop! You're killing a genius!

**John Gielgud missing his step while trying to board a
moving bus**

A narcissist is someone better looking than you are.

Gore Vidal

Warren Beatty is the type of man who will end up dying in his own arms.

Mamie Van Doren

Invest in a three-way mirror with movable sides so you can see yourself all the way round. I had one specially made.

Minnie Driver, fashion tip in *Elle* magazine

Modesty in an actor is as fake as passion in a call girl.

Jackie Gleason

–Do you think you've learned from your mistakes?
–What mistakes?

Interviewer and Leslie Caron

In future, Kevin Costner should only appear in pictures that he directs himself. That way he can always be working with his favorite actor and his favorite director.

Kevin Reynolds, director of Waterworld

If you ask any of my leading ladies they would tell you that they loved me. They should, because they have all given their best performances of their lives opposite me.

Michael Douglas

THE LOOK

Al Jolson's ego was such that when he heard
applause for another star, he reacted as though he
had been robbed.

Henry Levin

When Al Jolson attends a wedding he wants to be the
bride and when he attends a funeral he wants to be
the corpse.

Lou Anthony

It was easy enough to make Jolson happy at home.
You just had to cheer him at breakfast, applaud
wildly at lunch, and give him a standing ovation at
dinner.

George Burns

If people don't sit at Chaplin's feet, he goes and
stands where they're sitting.

Herman Mankiewicz

–I can't work with Paddy Chayevsky. He's an
egomaniac.

–Then you should get on just fine.

Ken Russell and Vivian Russell, his wife

The movies is the only business where you can go
out front and applaud yourself.

Will Rogers

Most celebrities walk into a room and say, "Here I
am." Cary Grant walked in and said, "There you are."

Abigail Van Buren

You can't get spoiled if you do your own ironing.

Meryl Streep

I asked Bette Davis if she'd ever wanted to meet the Queen of England. "What for?" she snapped, "I am a queen."

Natalie Wood

Elizabeth Taylor isn't spoiled. I have often seen her pour her own champagne for breakfast.

Mike Todd

What's this? Take it away. It's enough that I am here.

Marlene Dietrich refusing the check in a restaurant

Ava Gardner, complaining that the Maître d' at Ciro's had not shown her and Frank Sinatra immediately to the best table, grumbled, "We had to tell him who we were." Sammy Davis, interested, enquired, "And who were you?"

Lisa Marchant

I have yet to see one completely unspoiled star, except for Lassie.

Edith Head

AGE

Maggie Smith used to have excellent skin. Have you seen her face lately? In a few more years, they'll have to unfold it to find out who she used to be.

Jeremy Brett

Only two things improve with age: wine and Susan Sarandon.

Boyd Farrow

I'm not really wrinkled—I just had a nap on a chenille spread.

Phyllis Diller

Sexpots age fast in Hollywood.

Sharon Stone

Keep looking at my eyes, dahling. My arse is like an accordion.

Tallulah Bankhead

–You're not photographing me as well as you used to.
–I'm sorry, Miss Dietrich, but I'm ten years older now.

Hal Mohr, cinematographer and Marlene Dietrich

–How did your meeting with the movie producer go?
–Terrific. He said I have the eyes of a 12-year-old, the complexion of a 20-year-old and the legs of a 25-year old.
–What about your 60-year-old cunt?
–You were never mentioned.

Ernest Borgnine and Ethel Merman, husband and wife

I'm now at the age where I've got to prove that I'm just as good as I never was.

Rex Harrison

At 20 it's fun to be crazy. At 50 it's kind of sad.

John Waters

I hope I never get so old I get religious.

Ingmar Bergman

My pubic hair is going gray. In a certain light you'd swear it was Stewart Granger down there.

Billy Connolly

Careful grooming may take 20 years off a woman's age, but you can't fool a flight of stairs.

Marlene Dietrich

Hollywood obits are regularly in the high 80s—these are people who live a long time, which is what happens if you don't smoke, you work out every day, you get your body fat awesomely low and you do only the best cocaine.

David Thomson

—Mr Wilder, you're 90 years of age. To what do you attribute your longevity?
—To bad luck mostly.

Reporter and Billy Wilder

The secret of staying young is to live honestly, eat slowly, and lie about your age.

Lucille Ball

LOVE

DATING

The worst thing I have to do on a date is pretend I haven't heard the line "I don't just like you because you're Jack Nicholson" before.

Jack Nicholson

I still remember sitting in a darkened movie theater with my arm around 17-year-old Mary Joe Ramussen, trying to get to first base. I can even remember the name of the film: The Lion King.

Steve Martin

There are women with whom you can discuss the molecular theory of light all evening, and at the end they will ask you what your birth sign is.

Roman Polanski

There are so many guys out here with huge egos. Still, I prefer Hollywood dating to the Welsh version. Where I come from it's, "Do you want a pint of Guinness and a packet of crisps? I've got a transit van in the car park." At least here I'm taken out for dates in a private jet.

Catherine Zeta Jones

I'm the modern, intelligent, independent-type woman. In other words, a girl who can't get a man.

Shelley Winters

I like to wake up every morning feeling a new man.

Jean Harlow

Nowadays, only animated Disney heroines are
allowed to find Mr Right.

Libby Gelman-Waxner

LOVE

Love conquers all things—except poverty and
toothache.

Mae West

Every man I've known has fallen in love with Gilda
and wakened with me.

Rita Hayworth

No matter how much a woman loved a man, it
would still give her a glow to see him commit suicide
for her.

H.L. Mencken

The words, "I love you" are really a question.

Meryl Streep

SEX

I like it. And it likes me.

Joan Crawford

I didn't invent sex—I just rediscovered it, uncovered it, and gave it a couple of definitions that Mr Webster never thought of.

Mae West

I've tried everything but coprophilia and necrophilia, and I like kissing the best.

John Waters

I think men believe what they see in the movies— that I am going to throw my head back and have an orgasm in two minutes. I have never done that. It is implausible.

Sharon Stone

Sex is like death, only after death you don't feel like a pizza.

Woody Allen

Sex is simply the business of the three people involved.

Tallulah Bankhead

I don't have sexual fantasies—but then I've had all the realities.

Mae West

There is less successful sex in Hollywood than in Wichita, Kansas. Hollywood, uninhibited center of venery, is more headquarters for impotence than stallion play.

Ben Hecht

They called Sammy Davis Jr "The Carpenter" because
he nailed every girl he met.

Itovise Davis, Mrs Sammy Davis Jr

Hell, if I'd jumped on all the dames I'm supposed to
have jumped on, I'd have had no time to go fishing.

Clark Gable

If I had as many love affairs as I've been given credit
for, I'd be in a jar in the Harvard Medical School.

Frank Sinatra

It is doubtful whether sex played a more vital role in
Hollywood than it did in any large department store
or Eastern advertising business.

Budd Shulberg

I only have two rules for my newly born daughter:
she will dress well; she will never have sex.

John Malkovich

After Last Tango in Paris, waiters in restaurants
would bring me butter with a funny smile.

Marlon Brando

Husbands are chiefly good as lovers when they are
betraying their wives.

Marilyn Monroe

Whatever happened to the days when sex was Celia
Johnson and Rachmaninov on the piano?

Hugh Grant

MARRIAGE

In Hollywood, marriage is a success if it outlives milk.

Rita Rudner

What's the hardest thing for one actor to say to another? "Happy golden wedding anniversary, darling."

Jay Leno

Movie stars and monogamy go together like cornflakes and Tabasco.

Julia Llewellyn Smith

I find it impossible to conceive of spending a whole day with someone let alone getting married.

Christian Bale

Marry me and you'll be farting through silk for the rest of your days.

Robert Mitchum proposing

When Fernando Lamas proposed to me, he said, "Let me take you away from all this." And I said, "Away from all what? I'm a movie star!"

Esther Williams

My marriage license reads, "To whom it may concern."

Mickey Rooney, married 8 times

–How do you envisage married life will be?
–Long and hard, dahling. Long and hard.

Reporter and Tallulah Bankhead

Getting married is just the first step towards getting divorced.

Zsa Zsa Gabor

Marry an outdoor woman. Then if you throw her out in the yard for the night, she can still survive.

W.C. Fields

I wouldn't be caught dead married to a woman old enough to be my wife.

Tony Curtis

You may marry the man of your dreams, ladies, but 14 years later you're married to a couch that burps.

Roseanne

My mother gave me this advice: trust your husband, adore your husband and get as much as you can in your own name.

Joan Rivers

Mother told me a couple of years ago, "Sweetheart, settle down and marry a rich man." I said, "Mom, I am a rich man."

Cher

Peter Sellers had four wives and eight heart attacks.

John Frank-Keyes

I've had friends who when they marry say, "I know we're going to have to work at it." I always think they're wrong. The things that are really pleasurable in life, whether it's playing softball or working on your stamp collection, really require no effort.

Woody Allen

I planned on having one husband and seven children, but it turned out the other way around.

Lana Turner

I married four women eight times or is that eight women four times, I can never quite remember.

Stan Laurel

I've married a few people I shouldn't have, but haven't we all?

Mamie Van Doren

Of course I married Artie Shaw. Everybody married Artie Shaw!

Ava Gardner

You have no idea of the women I didn't marry.

Artie Shaw

–How long have we been married?
–Nearly four years.
–My God, I never meant to stay married to you that long!

Joan Fontaine and Brian Aherne

I think every woman's entitled to a middle husband she can forget.

Adela Rogers St Johns

A wife lasts only for the length of the marriage, but an ex-wife is there for the rest of your life.

Woody Allen

Married, I've been. Now I simply rent.

Frank Sinatra

Many a man owes his success to his first wife—and his second wife to his success.

Jim Backus

It is very difficult to be taken seriously when you're introduced at a party to somebody as the fourth Mrs Rex Harrison.

Rachel Roberts

Elizabeth succeeded Rachel Roberts as wife number five—the Catherine Howard part.

Rex Harrison

—What was life like as Mr Tallulah Bankhead?
—Like the rise, decline and fall of the Roman Empire.

Time **magazine and John Emery**

I'm living with a girl, but we're not married. It's kinda like leasing with an option to buy.

Jack Nicholson

Basically, the way it works now is that only the gay people get married in LA. Straight people don't bother anymore.

Craig Chester

DIVORCE

All the lines of dialogue in Natural Born Killers are things Oliver yelled at me. It's my divorce up there on screen.

Elizabeth Stone

I'm not upset about my divorce. I'm only upset I'm not a widow.

Roseanne

Roseanne went on Saturday Night Live and said I had a 3-inch penis. Well, even a 747 looks small if it's landing in the Grand Canyon.

Tom Arnold, ex-husband

A TV host asked my wife, "Have you ever considered divorce?" She replied, "Divorce never, murder often."

Charlton Heston

There's a group for men in Hollywood called Divorce Anonymous. It works like this: if a member of the group starts to feel the urge to divorce, they send over an accountant to talk him out of it.

Sean Connery

After my first wife and I were divorced, Alfred
Hitchcock expressed an interest in the movie rights
to the marriage.

Woody Allen

I think I shall risk the halibut. It can't be too awful,
can it? After you've lived with Laurence Harvey,
nothing in life is ever really too awful again.

Hermione Baddeley

I never speak of my ex-husbands except under
hypnosis.

Joan Collins

Why do Hollywood divorces cost so much? Because
they're worth it.

Johnny Carson

Julia Roberts and Lyle Lovett broke up this week.
Roberts says that for her, the marriage was over
when she realized, "I'm Julia Roberts, and he's Lyle
Lovett."

Norm MacDonald

FRIENDSHIP

Most of my fellow picture stars I only know well
enough to sneer at.

Constance Bennett

The monster was the best friend I ever had.

Boris Karloff

273

Ben Affleck is my best friend. He's the first guy I'd
call if I woke up in a hotel room with a dead hooker.

Matt Damon

Michael Winner is more than just a best friend to
me, he's a complete stranger.

Arnold Schwarzenegger at the opening of Planet Hollywood
restaurant in London

You can talk about love all you want. To me you're
nothing but a fucking dollar sign.

Dean Martin to Jerry Lewis on ending their partnership

Every film is like an ocean voyage, a transatlantic
crossing. You swear you will meet each other again,
but you never do.

George Sanders

Hollywood...where a producer loves you to death
until the end of the job and can't recognize you on
the street the next day.

Raymond Chandler

You can't find true affection in Hollywood because
everyone does the fake affection so well.

Carrie Fisher

The only friends I have in this goddamned town are
Haig & Haig.

John Barrymore

HOLLYWOOD
WISDOM

–How do you get into the movie business?
–Quit now.

Interviewer and David Zucker

–How do you get into the film business?
–You have to wait until someone dies and there is a vacancy.

Reporter and Steve Martin

There is only one way to get into pictures if you have as little talent as I have: you have to know someone.

Don Siegel

It's not who you know. It's who knows you.

Hollywood maxim

It's not who you know, it's who you blow.

Hollywood starlets' maxim

A starlet needs more than just looks. She needs idiocy too.

Clive James

In Hollywood, a girl's virtue is much less important than her hairdo.

Marilyn Monroe

If you want something done right, you have to do it yourself, as O.J. Simpson says.

Denis Leary

Life is a long rehearsal for a film that is never made.

Marlene Dietrich

–Can you explain the meaning of life?
–I can't, but I can dance it for you.

Interviewer and Woody Allen

–Is life worth living?
–That depends on the liver.

Reporter and W.C. Fields

Three things have helped me successfully through
the ordeals of life: an understanding husband, a
good analyst, and millions of dollars.

Mary Tyler Moore

Never play cards with a man named Doc. Never eat
at a place called Mom's. And never, no matter what
else you do in your whole life, never sleep with a
woman whose troubles are worse than your own.

Nelson Algren

Never sign a term contract with anyone who's
liable to grow more than 24 inches, perpendicularly
or horizontally, within the term of the aforesaid
contract.

Stanley Donen

Never pass a bathroom.

George Burns

Always wear shoes you can run away in.

Kym Barrett

Add 15 inches to your stride and save 41% of insects.

Courtney Love, a Buddhist

Trust in Allah, but tie up your camel.

Hollywood proverb

Whatever it is, be against it.

Humphrey Bogart to Robert Mitchum

My motto now that I'm getting old is if I wake up in the morning then I'm ahead for the day.

Mace Neufeld, producer

Adam West gave me some advice on how to wear the batsuit. He said, "Plan bathroom stops carefully. And beware of flushing your cape as you will strangle."

Val Kilmer

Quiet! I'm trying to travel!

Maureen Lipman to fellow train passengers chattering on cellphones

In Hollywood you don't have happiness. You send out for it.

Rex Reed

Having fun in Hollywood means running someone around the room, preferably someone more talented and less powerful than you.

Julia Phillips

Life is difficult enough without Meryl Streep movies.

Truman Capote

I have carried a whoopee cushion with me since 1975. It's a great ice-breaker.

Lesley Nielsen

The three most beautiful words in the English language are not, "I love you." They are, "It's benign."

Woody Allen

You can fool all the people some of the time, and some of the people all the time, but you can't fool Mom.

Mel Brooks

Whenever I wear something expensive it looks stolen.

Billy Connolly

–Look what your little dog's done–made a mess in my cab.

–It wasn't him, it was me.

Taxi-driver and Mrs Patrick Campbell

Edith Evans bought an incredibly expensive Renoir and, when a friend asked her why she had hung it so low on the wall, out of the light behind a curtain, she replied: "Because there was a hook."

Stephen Fry

Horse sense is what a horse has that keeps him from betting on people.

W.C. Fields

It's a 'mine's bigger than yours' mentality in
Hollywood. When John Travolta began bragging to
Spielberg about his new Gulf Stream Jet, Spielberg
interjected: "Yeah, but we don't have to duck our
heads in mine."

Laura Baum

I'm not the untidy person I played in The Odd Couple
but I'm not neat either. Which reminds me of a
story: A fellow gets married and the morning after
the wedding night, goes to the bathroom and finds a
dead horse in the bathtub. He runs out and says,
"Darling, there's a dead horse in the bathtub." And
his wife replies, "Well, I never said I was neat."

Walter Matthau

In airplanes, why is there a lifejacket and not a
parachute under the seat? And why is there no
window in the toilet—who on earth is going to see in?

Billy Connolly

How difficult can it be to fly a plane? I mean, John
Travolta learned how.

Graham Chapman

I married first, won the Oscar before Olivia did, and
if I die first she'll undoubtedly be livid because I beat
her to it.

Joan Fontaine on her sister, Olivia de Havilland

Everyone is fiercely competitive in Hollywood. I recall a dinner conversation with Michael Eisner in which I mentioned that I, like Eisner, had recently undergone bypass surgery. "Of course, mine was more serious," Eisner fired back.

John Gregory Dunne

My parents are great role models for me. Thanks to them, I certainly know how not to raise a child.

Drew Barrymore

If you make a movie with a male star, everyone assumes you're fucking. If it's a female star, everyone assumes you're fighting.

Susan Sarandon

On-set romances go with the territory. If you took two people who work in a bank and made them stand there saying "I love you" every morning, really trying to mean it, eventually they might start to believe it.

Jennifer Ehle

In America we have movie stars, tough guys like Jack Nicholson, Robert De Niro. In England, you get real human beings.

Woody Allen

Most British actors I have known would likely sell body parts to have a more lucrative career in Hollywood.

Alec Baldwin

I mean, what is the British Film Industry anyway? Just a bunch of people in London who can't get Green Cards.

Alan Parker, cartoon caption

I played Bernard Shaw's Saint Joan at the Los Angeles Music Center. The *LA Times* critic commented, "This is not one of Shakespeare's better plays."

Sarah Miles

I'm never going to write my autobiography as long as I live.

Samuel Goldwyn

I won't write my autobiography. Who cares how a writer got his first bicycle?

Raymond Chandler

I think I really wanted to write my biography to be able to mention that Jack Kennedy and I were friends more than anything else.

Jerry Lewis

Jackets not required but breast implants preferred.
Los Angeles Times, **Malibu restaurant review**

The quality of food in a restaurant is in inverse proportion to the number of signed celebrity photographs on the wall.

Bryan Miller

Planet Hollywood has filed for bankruptcy. Who would have thought the idea of an $18 hamburger wouldn't catch on?

Jay Leno, 1999

Basically, there are two types of exercise in LA: jogging, and helping a recently divorced friend move.

Robert Wagner

–Just look at that woman. She's practically a skeleton.

–Oh, Truman, that's anorexia nervosa.

–Oh, darling, you know everyone.

Truman Capote and friend

I have a punishing workout regimen. Every day I do three minutes on a treadmill, then I lie down, drink a glass of vodka and smoke a cigarette.

Anthony Hopkins

–Happy 103rd Birthday, Mr Zukor. What's the secret of your long life?

–I gave up smoking two years ago.

Interviewer and Adolph Zukor

I stopped smoking because I would wake up in the
middle of the night thinking I could hear burglars
downstairs. But it was only my bronchial chords
making a din.

Peter Ustinov

In Hollywood, it's more acceptable for a bar owner to
possess a firearm than an ashtray.

Will Buckley

All literature is a footnote to Faust. I have no idea
what I mean by that.

Woody Allen

In the theater I'm playing, there's a hole in the wall
between the ladies' dressing room and mine. I've
been meaning to plug it up, but what the hell...let
'em enjoy themselves.

George Burns

--What is your greatest regret?
--Not knowing at 30 what I knew about women at 60.

Interviewer and Arthur Miller

You don't know a woman until you've met her in
court.

Woody Allen

A man has to be Saddam Hussein to be called
ruthless. All a woman has to do is put you on hold.

Bette Midler

If a man does something silly, people say, "Isn't he silly?" If a woman does something silly, people say, "Aren't women silly?"

Doris Day

When a man gives his opinion, he's a man. When a woman gives her opinion she's called a bitch.

Demi Moore

Jail? It's just like Palm Springs without the riffraff.

Robert Mitchum, jailed on drugs charges

I play a lot of golf and someone once asked me what my handicap was. I said, "I'm a colored, one-eyed Jew—do I need anything else?"

Sammy Davis Jr

Woody Allen always insisted that my lips remain tight closed during kissing scenes. He kept his clothes on under the sheet, and he even kept his shoes on too. When I asked him why, he said, "In case there's a fire."

Helena Bonham Carter on Mighty Aphrodite

The men in Hollywood? They're either married, going through divorce or want to do your hair.

Doris Day

-- You know who runs Hollywood?
--The Jews?
--No, the gay Jews.

Hollywood joke

Take out all the homosexuals and there is no
Hollywood.

Elizabeth Taylor

My mother was always warning me to be careful of
theatrical types and never to turn my back.

Michael Crawford

Father warned me about men, but he never said anything about women.

Tallulah Bankhead

Just as in real estate it's "location, location, location,"
the formula for showbiz success is "lesbians, lesbians,
lesbians."

Howard Stern

When I check into a hotel, I pull out the Gideon's
Bible and rip out the part of Leviticus that says people
like me should be removed from the face of the earth.

Sir Ian McKellen

Popcorn is the last area of movie business where
good taste is still a concern.

Vincent Canby

Popcorn is such a loud food. I urge movie theater
owners to rethink movie food and sell something
quieter. Maybe bags of sliced tomatoes.

Rita Rudner

The beauty of subtitled films is that you can crunch your way through a bumper family pack of tortilla chips without missing any dialogue.

Kirk Jones

There came a point where I had to stop trying to shock or I'd have ended up making a film about people eating the contents of their own colostomy bags.

John Waters

Sometimes I'm not sure there's ever been an America. I just think it's all been Frank Capra films.

John Cassavetes

There is a difference between American and European films. American films usually involve a car chase while European films usually involve a small boy and a bicycle.

Boyd Farrow

Good movies rarely contain a hot-air balloon.

Roger Ebert

Bad taste is simply saying the truth before it should be said.

Mel Brooks

A cult film is a movie seen about 50 times by about that many people.

Rick Bayan

My name is Francis Coppola. I am dropping the
Ford. This comes from a statement I once heard:
"Never trust a man who has three names."

Francis Coppola

Having a double-barreled name merely makes it hell
signing autographs.

Helena Bonham Carter

When your name ends in a vowel, you end up
carrying a gun a lot.

Anthony LaPaglia on being cast in gangster roles

The stupidest question I've ever been asked is
whether Hermione Gingold is my real name. Now I
just say, "Not really. I was born Norma Jean Baker."

Hermione Gingold

Dick Van Dyke? We know him as Penis Lorry Lesbian.

Stephen Fry

Sarah Michelle, Melissa Joan, Sarah Jessica, Charlize,
Keri—young actresses today all seem to have been
named after centerfolds or moisturizers.

Libby Gelman-Waxner

Although we all like to think that cinema is the most
important culture on earth, we are fooling ourselves
in the same way Charlton Heston is each morning
when he sticks a Shredded Wheat on his head.

Boyd Farrow

I thought you played around with Lauren Bacall for a little while, then you met Doris Day and settled down. Boy, was I wrong! That's the lie movies gave to me.

Henry Jaglom

I don't go to the movies. Maybe it's the same as not eating hot dogs after you've worked in a slaughter house. You know it's all made from ears and ass parts.

Harrison Ford

From the movies we learn precisely how to hold a champagne flute, kiss a mistress, pull a trigger, turn a phrase... but the movies spoil us for life; nothing ever lives up to them.

Edmund White

I prefer television to movies. It's not so far to the bathroom.

Fred Allen

End credits have become completely absurd. There was one movie...where the credits went on and on. I happened to be tired and just sat there. And one of the credit lines was, "If you'd left at the beginning of these credits, you'd be home now."

Andrew Sarris

Actors never retire. They're just offered less and less work.

David Niven

I won't quit the business until I get run over by a truck, a producer or a critic.

Jack Lemmon

When I told my daughter that Edith Evans had died, she said, "I don't believe it. She's not the type."

Brian Forbes

I know what they'll put on my tombstone: Here lies Herm—I mean Joe Mankiewicz.

Joseph L. Mankiewicz

It's very sad. A silver bell has been silenced.

George Peppard on the death of Audrey Hepburn

Bury me in the garden, in the center of the croquet lawn, Robert said. This disturbed me because I am a croquet fanatic and it would interfere with my game.

Sarah Miles on husband, Robert Bolt's last wishes

Gary Cooper. William Holden. Ty Power. Gloria Swanson. Humphrey Bogart. Erich von Stroheim. Marilyn Monroe. Eddie Robinson. Charles Laughton. Man, what a picture He could cast up there— with a score by Beethoven, naturally, and sets by Michelangelo, and additional dialogue by William Shakespeare. And, of course, ultimately, it will all wind up in turnaround.

Billy Wilder

INDEX